Meeting Girls Like Us

Meeting Girls Like Us

—m—

Old Testament Women

Book 2

Barby Bailey

Dedication

Although this book is written to women, it is lovingly dedicated to the three most important men in my life:

To Mark, my husband of 45 years: What an adventure we have enjoyed, my love! You keep me laughing. You support me in all my endeavors. You are my go-to resident Bible scholar. You make my world secure and I love you for it!

To Josh, our firstborn: You are my favorite minister of music and I marvel at how beautifully you conduct the choir and orchestra, always lifting my heart in worship. I love the ways you serve our Lord, our church, and your family; always with joy.

To Jeremy, our lastborn: You are my favorite football coach and I marvel at the impact of your ministry with those you coach and teach. I love your heart for the Lord and His Word, always growing in your knowledge and application.

Preface

I never started out to write a book, nor did I dream I ever would. This project began some years ago when I developed an interest in the women in Scripture and taught about them at several retreats, conferences, and in different church settings. After numerous comments from those who heard the lessons, advising me to put this content in a book, I took their encouragement as from the Lord. So here we are.

As I studied these women in depth, I discovered they were just like me. Women are women, no matter the century or the culture. We share the same hormones, emotions, and female brain characteristics. I identified with their responses to the circumstances and relationships they encountered.

In developing their stories, only extrapolating what the Bible said about them, my passion became to introduce these girls in a fresh way to women today. I want to link our lives to theirs to better understand them. To that end, this book is just the beginning.

My prayer is that this tool can be used, not only for informational purposes, but also for spiritual growth, as the focus points at the end of each chapter will help apply God's truth to our everyday lives.

Acknowledgements

To my girls, Emily and Callie: my own beloved daughters-in-law. I could fill a book with all the ways I love and appreciate you both. Suffice it to say that you are God's love gifts to me. You love my sons well. You are raising godly children. You are beautiful, classy, and so much fun! You teach me about myself and help connect me with your generation. My life is infinitely better because of you two lovelies!

To the mothers of my girls: Sara Jo and Amy. Girlfriends, you raised marvelous girls who are following in your footsteps and making all of us proud. I am forever grateful that God joined our families together. Thank you for being such excellent role models to your daughters. Thank you for loving God with all your hearts. Thank you for praying so faithfully for our kids. It is pure joy to share grandchildren with you both. I love you!

To my sister, Grace: You were my first answer to a six-yearrr-old's nightly prayer. Having three wonderful brothers did not mean I wanted a fourth! The night you were born, Dad woke me up with the words, "Honey, God has answered your prayer. You have a baby sister!" You excel as a pastor's wife, Mom, Grammy, Spanish teacher,

Bible teacher and role model for all who know you. I love you forever, baby girl.

To my sisters by marriage: Carol, Joy, Marlene, Marijean, and Judy. You girls are my heart-sisters. Each of you has impacted me in meaningful ways and I am grateful. I love our times together, filled with laughter, and sometimes tears. I am thankful that our bond goes beyond the ordinary. You are precious to me.

To my new sister in Christ: Theresa, what a joy it has been to behold your transformation! I knew you before you became a believer and have witnessed the difference Jesus makes in everything! I have loved discipling you and am thrilled you are a member of our church, active in a home group, and going through BSF. How fun to share a birthday with you, my precious friend!

To my content editor: Margaret Tolliver. This book would never have happened without your expert guidance, deep insights, thought-provoking questions, and generous encouragement. You were courageous enough to challenge me in ways that caused me to dig deeper and I am richer for it.

To my copy editor: Kathy Dyer. I went to school through all your expert edits, and I now know the difference between hyphens, en-dashes, and em-dashes. I feel so empowered! Thank you for your treasured friendship, and for your encouragement, my dear compadre in ministry.

Table of Contents

I

Naomi: Seeking Security

Picture lounging comfortably on the deck of a boat tied securely to a pier. The warm sunshine caresses your face, the cooling breeze bathes your body, and gentle waves lull you into blissful relaxation. But suddenly, the ropes come undone, the sun hides behind a darkening cloud, the breeze chills, and choppy waves begin to batter your boat, pulling you out to sea.

Stormy circumstances beyond our control can threaten our strong need for security. If our security rests in the seaworthiness of the boat, or our skill as a watercraft operator, we might be in serious trouble when battling fierce storms. When resources are exhausted, and human efforts to control unpredictable events fail, we begin to feel insecure and defeated. One writer asks and answers an all-important question as it relates to our security. "Where does your security lie? Is God your refuge, your hiding place, your stronghold, your shepherd, your counselor, your friend, your redeemer, your Savior, your guide? If He is, you don't need to search any further for security."[1]

As we unpack Naomi's story in this chapter, we will meet a woman whose life-storms challenged her sense of security and set her world spinning out of control. We will watch her grapple with famine, homelessness, death, and poverty. Because she transparently and honestly shared her deepest feelings when her "boat" became unmoored and tossed wildly in raging seas, we will learn valuable lessons from this ancient sister who has much to teach us.

"Now it came about in the days when the judges governed, that there was a famine in the land" (Ruth 1:1a). Naomi's story, shrouded in somber tones, becomes more ominous as it progresses. Uncertainty ruled the day in this era when sequential judges governed. Except for times of intermittent peace, the people of Israel faced enemy attacks preventing them from planning their future, forcing them to live in a panicky climate of fear. The book of Ruth follows the book of Judges in the Old Testament, so it's important to note the final verse in Judges, which aptly summed up Naomi's reality. "In those days there was no king in Israel; everyone did what was right in his own eyes" (Judges 21:25). Without a righteous king such as David, or Josiah, to govern according to God's law, anarchy and chaos erupted as people created their own rules.

To be labeled as such, a region in famine must be experiencing extreme scarcity of food resulting in widespread hunger, even starvation. It is usually caused by crop failure or other natural disaster. God, in control of all the elements of His creation, had warned His people of the dire consequences resulting from disobedience to His laws. One of the ways His divine discipline expressed itself was through rainfall, specifically the lack thereof, when He warned His people, "The Lord will make the rain of your land powder and dust" (Deuteronomy 28:24).

Women who pride themselves on obtaining food for their families, and who rely upon a peaceful climate in which to raise secure children, would be stretched and stressed to human capacity. Suffering through this terrible famine, we can imagine Naomi spending long hours scrounging for food and doling it out carefully, leaving her mentally, emotionally, and physically exhausted. We can picture her becoming gaunt and weak, denying her own needs to sacrificially feed her two boys. When the famine worsened and food supplies dwindled drastically, Naomi and her husband made the difficult choice to flee their homeland.

"And a certain man of Bethlehem in Judah went to sojourn in the land of Moab with his wife and his two sons" (Ruth 1:1b). Bethlehem means *house of bread,* or in a broader sense, *house of food.*[2] How ironic that a town known for its abundance of food, especially bread, would succumb to a complete lack of it! It's unlikely that Naomi's husband intended to permanently leave Bethlehem to live in Moab. The word *sojourn* has the idea of visiting a place or becoming a temporary resident in another city for a certain amount of time. We surmise that the family fully intended to return to Bethlehem once the famine had ceased and bread became abundant once more.

Naomi's husband chose to relocate his family to Moab, a region east of Israel across the Dead Sea. Moab, modern-day central/eastern Jordan, measured about fifty miles from Bethlehem.[3] To us, fifty miles is not much considering our options in modern transportation. However, to a family with children, walking that many miles across challenging terrain would have been no small feat for little feet. Why Moab? Perhaps they had relatives living there, or maybe they simply sought refuge in a neighboring famine-free region.

Traveling in that part of the world, surveying the terrain, I have often wondered how Naomi managed to cross the Dead Sea from Israel into Moab. Full of salt, and other caustic minerals, this body of water is not at all hospitable to boats, rafts, or swimmers. One writer speculated that the family "may have traveled southward to Hebron, descended eastward to the Dead Sea, crossed the sea to the Lisan (the land peninsula that extends into the Dead Sea) and climbed into the interior of Moab. This would have been the shortest route to Moab."[4]

Israel and Moab engaged in skirmishes during the period of the judges. However, there were also times of truce between the two nations. It would have been difficult, if not infeasible; to move to Moab during a war, so perhaps the two nations enjoyed a peaceful period when Naomi's family sought refuge from the famine. Transitioning from Israel to Moab would have been eased by not having to learn a foreign language, as the two nations shared many similarities in that regard.[5] The Moabites, a Semitic people group, descended from Lot, Abraham's nephew, and their language closely resembled Hebrew.

So Naomi, her husband, Elimelech, and their two boys, Mahlon and Chilion, "entered the land of Moab and remained there" (Ruth 1:2). In Naomi's day, names held special significance and often told a story about the person. Elimelech means *my God is king*. "The narrator's explicit identification of his name seems to cast him in a positive light."[6] Naomi means *sweetness*, or *pleasantness*. Mahlon means *sickly* and Chilion means *frail*.[7] Often, due to high infant mortality rates, parents typically did not name babies until it appeared they would survive through infancy. Perhaps Naomi and Elimelech named their two sons to reflect the rough start they had in life, or even to describe their weak condition due to the famine.[8]

While residing in Moab, tragedy struck. "Then Elimelech, Naomi's husband, died; and she was left with her two sons" (Ruth 1:3). Naomi must have been so frightened and devastated, away from home, without the love and support of her husband. If she had felt insecure before due to the severe famine in her homeland, she would have felt doubly insecure now, alone with two sons in a foreign land with no visible means of support.

On one occasion, my husband, Mark, and I traveled to Turkey. We didn't know that right before we left home, Mark had been exposed to a nasty virus. After a few days in Istanbul, Mark succumbed to this hard-hitting infection. As he worsened considerably, we separated from our tour group, choosing to stay behind in a hotel to see if he would get better. With Mark confined to bed, I remember feeling unsettled, far from home in this foreign land. One frightening night is etched in my memory. Mark, coughing incessantly, suddenly stopped breathing and began to turn blue. In full panic mode, I pounded his chest and yelled his name; fearing I was losing him. Thankfully, he revived. After the shock of his losing consciousness for a few seconds, he almost had to revive me! We made the decision that night to return home. In God's providence, we booked a return flight and obtained medical clearance to fly. Within twenty-four hours, we were back home. Naomi had no such recourse available to her. She mourned her husband's loss in this foreign land without the support of her loving community back in Bethlehem.

Elimelech passed away before his sons married. Perhaps he had planned on waiting to marry off his boys until the family could return to Bethlehem to find Israelite wives. His unfortunate and untimely passing must have altered many plans as the small family adjusted to the shock. We are not told how long after Elimelech died that his sons "took for themselves Moabite women as wives; the name of the one was Orpah and the name of the other Ruth. And they lived there about ten years" (Ruth 1:4). Interestingly, the name Orpah means *back of the neck* or *to turn one's back,* and Ruth means *friend* or *female companion.*[9] Naomi's fatherless sons, by now acclimated to the region, may have assumed they'd be living in Moab indefinitely and, as such, wanted to move on with their lives to establish families of their own.

The demise of her husband created upheaval in all parts of Naomi's life, particularly when it came to arranging marriages for her two sons. Ordinarily, the father of sons would handle the wedding arrangements. In that culture, the bridegroom, rather than the bride, received the most attention during all the festivities. The father would pay the bride price, determine the day of the wedding, and preside over all the celebrations.[10] As the reluctant head of her household, Naomi had to make decisions and finalize details normally outside her realm of control. In addition, she needed to consider local customs as she planned a Jewish wedding for her sons. She may have worked to appease her foreign daughters-in-law. After all, they would be living with her. In Naomi's era, it was customary for a married son to bring his wife home to live with his parents. Many Middle Eastern families carry on this tradition today as well.

Mosaic law did not prohibit an Israelite man from marrying a Moabitess. However, God did forbid intermarrying with several other listed Canaanite people groups as recorded in Deuteronomy 7:1–3. Intermarrying with them was prohibited on the assumption that the Israelites would be tempted to adopt pagan gods and all the perverted practices that accompanied the false worship of them. In addition, "the law forbade Moabite males from joining the assembly of the Lord (Deuteronomy 23:3)."[11] Interestingly, before the fall of Jerusalem to Rome, Jewish lineage was always patrilineal. In biblical times, "Judaism was passed on by the father, not the mother. A quick glance at Biblical genealogies makes this clear – see the many examples of Jewish kings who took non-Jewish spouses – and in inter-tribal marriage during the Biblical era, paternal descent was likewise decisive. A non-Jewish woman marrying a Jewish man didn't even have to convert. She was now part of the tribe and her children would naturally be Jewish."[12] If Naomi's sons' marriages produced offspring, the children would be considered Jewish through the father's lineage. "Even though they were foreigners, they had married Israelite men and thus were under God's covenant."[13] So Ruth married Mahlon (Ruth 4:10), and Orpah married Chilion.

Unfortunately, Naomi's bereavement compounded twofold. "Then both Mahlon and Chilion also died, and the woman was bereft of her two children and her husband" (Ruth 1:5). Only those who have suffered the loss of husband and children can fathom the depths of this dear woman's grief. According to how Naomi's sons are referenced in the text, it may be that they died at the same time or close together. The word *bereft* has the connotation of deprivation, or of being robbed. After Elimelech died, Naomi's desire for security hinged upon her two sons, and the joyful prospect of grandchildren to soften her pain and enliven her old age. With the unexpected, untimely death of her two precious boys, Naomi must have been engulfed in a suffocating cloud of dark and bitter grief that felt endless. This devastating loss of husband and sons, without the network of loving support Naomi had left behind in her homeland, certainly made life incredibly difficult for this sorrow-ravaged woman. She wasn't completely alone, however. Her daughters-in-law were still considered part of her family even though their husbands had died, so they resided with Naomi. How wonderful that Naomi did not have to grieve all alone. She could share the heavy burden of her grief with two girls who also loved her sons.

Grieving together over the loss of the men they loved would have helped the three women form a tight bond, even though they didn't worship the same God. As native Moabites, Ruth and Orpah carried pagan beliefs and practices with them into Naomi's home. The Moabites' principal god was Chemosh, a fish-god, whose name means *destroyer* or *subduer*.[14] The two girls would have observed

Naomi grieving in the context of her faith and hope in the God of Israel, and perhaps that presented a stark contrast to them.

Naomi emerged from the arduous grieving process with enough drive to make big decisions, which is truly remarkable. Anyone who has suffered the loss of a loved one knows that grief cannot be rushed nor circumvented. It takes its necessary toll in time and tears. "Then she arose with her daughters-in-law that she might return from the land of Moab, for she had heard in the land of Moab that the Lord had visited His people in giving them food" (Ruth 1:6). Naomi may have been physically cut off from her homeland, but news still traveled from Israel into Moab. The end of the famine signaled welcome news indeed! Relief in the form of rain could be directly attributed to God blessing His chosen people to give them food. As Naomi relayed the news to her daughters-in-law, perhaps she recognized God's role in lifting the famine and, if so, she may have better appreciated His loving provision of food for them. This good news gave Naomi something joyful to celebrate and helped penetrate her veil of grief with a shaft of bright light. She now had hope that she could return home.

As permanent fixtures in Naomi's life, joined to her through their husbands, the girls prepared to return with her to Bethlehem. "So she departed from the place where she was, and her two daughters-in-law with her; and they went on the way to return to the land of Judah" (Ruth 1:7). Honoring the practice of their day, both Orpah and Ruth fully intended to live the rest of their lives with Naomi instead of returning to their own mothers. We can only imagine how heart-rending it must have been for these two girls to say good-bye to everything familiar, including their own families, and head off with their mother-in-law into uncharted territory. In addition, Naomi would have been torn between returning home and leaving behind the graves of her husband and sons.

Earlier, she had navigated the difficult trek to Moab under the protection of her husband and in the joyful company of her sons. Now, she resolved to undertake the journey as a bereaved widow in charge of two dependent daughters-in-law. Naomi would never have contemplated the daunting task of returning to Bethlehem had she not been confident that God would protect her and provide the resources she needed. We don't know how far the three women traveled before Naomi said to her two daughters-in-law, "Go, return each of you to her mother's house" (Ruth 1:8).

Naomi loved these girls enough to release them from the marriage vows binding them to her. She loved these girls enough to desire the happiness that reuniting with their own mothers would bring. A mother-in-law can never take the place of a mother in a daughter-in-law's life, nor should she. The ultimate blessing for any mother-in-law is the sweet friendship and kind, loving relationship she can enjoy with her daughter-in-law. Apparently, Naomi and her two daughters-in-law were blessed in that regard because she said to them, "May the Lord deal kindly with you as you have dealt with the dead and with me" (Ruth 1:8).

These girls became a blessing to Naomi. They were kind to her sons, and kind to her. Considering the extent of her sorrow, Naomi's loving and kind relationship with her two daughters-in-law certainly helped buoy her spirits on those days when grief felt like a heavy hand pressing down on her. The fact that Naomi desired the Lord to deal kindly with her daughters-in-law implies that she had shared knowledge about her God with them. Naomi wanted the girls to know that God is good, and capable of dealing kindly with them, even when she regarded some of His dealings with her to be harsh and seemingly undeserved. Naomi wanted the girls to experience God's kindness as she had experienced His kindness in the form of her husband and two sons. The Hebrew word is *hesed*. It means *loyal love, unfailing kindness*, and *devotion*.[15] It's a love or affection that is steadfast and unconditional. We don't deserve God's *hesed* lavished on us continually, but He delights to enfold us in this amazing love.

I have thoroughly enjoyed my own two daughters-in-law for years now. I love them with all my heart, and they have been nothing but kind and loving to my sons and to me. Even when I say things I shouldn't, they are kind to me. Even when I attempt to control a situation to make me feel more comfortable, they are still kind to me. I realize that is not always the case. Some may suffer acrimonious relationships with a daughter-in-law. Yes, it's always an adjustment whenever a new family member is added, altering the family dynamic. Gaining a daughter-in-law necessitates a conscious, deliberate choice on our part. We can choose to welcome and love the new family member, or we can resent her, and look for copious reasons to find fault with her. We can allow ourselves to feel threatened by her, or decide to embrace her and learn to appreciate her "differentness." We can choose to lavish *hesed* on her the same way God lavishes it on us. While we were still sinners, God loved us. Even if our *hesed* is not appreciated or reciprocated, even if we feel it is not deserved or properly earned, that doesn't warrant our withdrawing of it. We never merited God's *hesed,* nor could we ever hope to earn it. If a daughter-in-law happens to be an unbeliever, or intent on making our lives difficult, what a great opportunity to be an expression of God's *hesed* and love her into the kingdom!

As mothers-in-law, we are blessed to become friends with our daughter-in-law, and even more blessed if that friendship deepens and she considers us one of her trusted mentors. As I've listened to many women complain about and criticize their daughters-in-law, I wonder if one of the underlying issues is our lack of control. We had no control over how she was raised. We had no control when our son fell in love with her. We have no control over how she treats our son, raises her children, or makes life choices. We can allow the way she relates to our son and how she raises our grandchildren to bother us because she is not doing it the way we would, or we can choose to look for all the good choices she makes and decide to affirm and encourage her.

In my own journey as a mother-in-law, I have been learning how to make allowances and reach a place of surrendered acceptance as outlined in the following commitments I made in my heart to my two daughters-in-law:

I accept that the close bond I have enjoyed with my son as the most important female in his life, will now need to flex and stretch, allowing ample room for a new most important female.

I accept my God-given calling to love my daughter-in-law with sacrificial and unconditional love because that is exactly how God loves me.

I accept my responsibility to pray for my daughter-in-law on a regular basis and earnestly desire God's best for her life.

I accept the role of conducting myself in God-glorifying ways in all conversations and situations. I choose to be a positive example of what it looks like to be a committed Christ-follower.

I accept the reality that disappointments and irritations are inherent within all human nature relationships, and so I choose to expect them and not allow the enemy to use them to derail my own walk of joy with the Lord.

I accept that my love for my daughter-in-law should not be based on how she looks, how she was raised, what she says, what activities she enjoys, how she spends her time, how she uses social

> *media, how she keeps house, or how she treats me. I choose my*
> *love to for her to reflect God's unfailing and unconditional love*
> *for me.*

Sadly, some mothers-in-law purposely alienate their daughter-in-law by maintaining a resentful attitude and indiscriminately expressing their criticism of her. These tactics only serve to undermine any efforts to build a good relationship with her and can sever coveted access to beloved grandchildren. These mothers-in-law don't realize, until it's sometimes too late, that by keeping a daughter-in-law at arm's length, outside her circle of loving acceptance, they have boxed themselves into a lonely room of their own making.

Equally sad, some daughters-in-law shun a relationship with their mother-in-law, choosing to remain estranged and distant. Perhaps the relationship started off on the wrong foot and continued to worsen. Whatever the cause or current state of affairs, Romans 12:9–18 offers wonderful advice to follow with God's help. " Don't just pretend to love others. Really love them. Hate what is wrong. Hold tightly to what is good. Love each other with genuine affection, and take delight in honoring each other. Never be lazy, but work hard and serve the Lord enthusiastically. Rejoice in our confident hope. Be patient in trouble, and keep on praying. When God's people are in need, be ready to help them. Always be eager to practice hospitality. Bless those who persecute you. Don't curse them; pray that God will bless them. Be happy with those who are happy, and weep with those who weep. Live in harmony with each other. Don't be too proud to enjoy the company of ordinary people. And don't think you know it all. Never pay back evil with more evil. Do things in such a way that everyone can see you are honorable. Do all that you can to live in peace with everyone" (NLT).

After encouraging her daughters-in-law to return to their own mothers, Naomi blessed them. "May the Lord enable each of you to find security in the home of a new husband" (Ruth 1:9, NET). Naomi addressed one of our most basic needs as women—security. When we feel insecure and unsafe, it's hard to fully enjoy any area of our lives. In Naomi's day, a husband and children spelled security for a woman and Naomi didn't want her husbandless, childless, insecure life for them. Nowadays, single women have so many more options than Naomi could have ever imagined. Due to a plethora of careers available to us, a full and rewarding life can be had, no matter the marital status, but only if one finds her true security and full contentment in the Lord.

In her prayer for her daughters-in-law, Naomi emphasized the role of God as our helper when she expressed her loving desire for them. She wanted them to know that God could grant them security by helping them find new husbands. Even though Naomi strongly encouraged her daughters-in-law to find Moabite men who most likely worshipped pagan deities, perhaps the alternative of remaining husbandless seemed an even greater evil to her. In her time, widowed women were especially vulnerable financially, physically, and emotionally as they struggled on the sidelines of male-dominated society. How it must have wrenched Naomi's heart to say good-bye to these kind and loving daughters-in-law who meant so much to her. How it must have stabbed her soul to imagine them finding new husbands and having children who would not be her own grandchildren. Her genuine love for them offered release from prior bonds at great cost to her. In that moment, Naomi loved them unconditionally and sacrificially, modeling God's *hesed* in a beautiful way.

"Then she kissed them, and they lifted up their voices and wept" (Ruth 1:9). Their loud weeping and genuine tears lent credence to their great love for each other as they envisioned a permanent separation. Up to this point in her story, Naomi's life consisted of one loss after another: her daily bread, her homeland, her husband, her sons, and now her beloved daughters-in-law. The women mourned the loss of each other, as well as the loss of future opportunities to deepen their mutual love and devotion. Naomi and her daughters-in-law recognized that, should they go their separate ways, a reunion in this life would be unlikely. Saying good-bye to each other probably felt like another death in this already death-ravaged family.

Unwilling to part with Naomi, both girls protested, "No, but we will surely return with you to your people" (Ruth 1:10). Given the chance to stay with their mothers, find new husbands, and remain in the familiar surroundings of Moab, the girls strongly expressed their desire to travel on with Naomi. Even if cultural norms dictated their passionate response, it still speaks so highly of Naomi! These daughters-in-law were not only kind and loving to Naomi, they were also loyally devoted to her. By her words and actions, Naomi had made it easy for these girls to love her. The girls' fervent affirmation must have warmed Naomi's heart. "But Naomi said, 'Return, my daughters. Why should you go with me? Have I yet sons in my womb, that they may be your husbands? Return, my daughters! Go, for I am too old to have a husband. If I said I have hope, if I should even have a husband tonight and also bear sons, would you therefore wait until they were grown? Would you therefore refrain from marrying? No, my daughters; for it is harder for me than for you, for the hand of the Lord has gone forth against me'" (Ruth 1:11–13).

In Naomi's equally passionate reply to her daughters-in-law, she asked four rhetorical questions which, based on the way they were phrased, demanded negative answers. Naomi's questions need to be considered in light of the levirate law under which all three operated.

"Naomi reminded them that she was not pregnant with sons who, as the younger brothers of Mahlon and Kilion, would be obligated to marry their widowed sisters-in-law according to the levirate law."[16] Naomi asked the girls to imagine the impossible, think through all their options, and then choose the logical path. She called Orpah and Ruth her "daughters" three times in this section, indicating her closeness to them, claiming them as her own. Naomi was more concerned about their future than her own. She loved them enough to place their needs above hers.

Studying Naomi's response to her daughters-in-law, it may appear that in contrasting her grief to theirs, she exhibited insensitivity by portraying her sorrow as greater. "Naomi seemed a bit insensitive to the grief of her daughters-in-law. She thought that her case was more bitter than theirs because they still had potential for childbearing. She regarded her plight as a result of God's affliction (cf. verses 20–21). Naomi was apparently in a stage of grief that caused her to speak in anger against God. And yet she was still a woman of faith. She had no doubt God was actively involved in their lives. She saw God as sovereign and the ultimate cause of life's issues."[17]

Naomi regarded her suffering as ongoing when she admitted her perception that the Lord was against her, afflicting her. Naomi didn't want her "daughters" to continue to align themselves with her intense suffering. She wanted them to have a reprieve from her unrelenting sorrow. Another translation reads, "For my intense suffering is too much for you to bear" (Ruth 1:13, NET). And yet, Naomi also portrayed God in a good light as she highlighted His concern and provision for people in famine (Ruth 1:6), His capacity for displaying *hesed* (Ruth 1:8), and His consideration of female needs for security (Ruth 1:9).

Sadly, Naomi's great despair over the way her life had turned out impacted her reasoning to some degree. By suggesting her daughters-in-law return to their foreign gods, Naomi was potentially depriving them of the ultimate blessing of knowing the God of Israel and making a personal choice about Him. However, it must be noted that Naomi's bitter experience, attributed to God's harsh dealing with her, did not prevent her from still seeking the Lord's blessing for her daughters-in-law, even as she encouraged them to stay in Moab. Underlying all Naomi's disappointments, there resided a firm belief in the existence of God and in His ability to sovereignly withhold or bestow His blessings.

After Naomi's forthright, but loving words, her daughters-in-law "lifted up their voices and wept again; and Orpah kissed her mother-in-law, but Ruth clung to her" (Ruth 1:14). At this critical juncture, a decision had to be made. Orpah chose to live up to her name, *turn one's back*, and after kissing Naomi good-bye, headed for home. This is the last we hear of Orpah. Ruth, on the other hand, clung to her mother-in-law, refusing to heed her advice and say good-bye. The word used here for "clung to," *dabaq*, elsewhere in Scripture refers to the ideal closeness that can be experienced in a marriage relationship.[18] Naomi told Ruth, "Behold, your sister-in-law has gone back to her people and her gods; return after your sister-in-law" (Ruth 1:15).

It's encouraging to know that despite Naomi's tragedy, subsequent bereavement, and life in Moab surrounded by pagan gods, her grief did not drive her to seek solace in them. She could have quite easily adopted Moab's gods as her own when she resided there; so many others had done just that in times of trouble. But Naomi remained steadfastly focused on *Yahweh,* the one true God. She never turned her back on Him. Orpah turned her back on that strong witness, but Ruth did not.

Ruth was fully aware she would be leaving her pagan gods to follow Naomi and her God. "In ancient times it was believed that a deity had power only in the geographical region occupied by his or her worshipers. Thus to leave one's land meant separation from one's gods."[19] Even though Naomi's statement indicated an incomplete theology of God, Ruth uttered a fervent declaration that certainly encouraged Naomi's heart. "Do not urge me to leave you or turn back from following you; for where you go, I will go, and where you lodge, I will lodge. Your people shall be my people, and your God, my God. Where you die, I will die, and there I will be buried. Thus may the Lord do to me, and worse, if anything but death parts you and me" (Ruth 1:16–17).

Ruth's all-in speech left Naomi speechless. When Naomi grasped Ruth's firm resolve to bind herself to her beloved mother-in-law for life, she had nothing more to say (Ruth 1:18). Ruth clung to Naomi, but even more importantly, she clung to Naomi's God. Perhaps she had embraced Naomi's faith while married to Mahlon. Or maybe she came to faith after his death. Whenever it happened, her public confession surely bolstered Naomi's heart. Ruth put her newfound belief into practice when she invoked the Lord to make sure she kept her promise to Naomi. Ruth lived up to the meaning of her name, *friend* or *female companion*, and promised to be that to Naomi for life. Ruth's wholesale allegiance to Naomi's God and Naomi's people clearly showcased a heart moved to place all her trust in the God of Israel. In deciding to follow Naomi, Ruth willingly forfeited any chance of finding a new husband and bearing children with him. She turned her back on everything women in her day valued to follow Naomi and embrace her faith.

In pledging allegiance to Naomi's God, Ruth joined herself to the Lord. As God promised, "Also the foreigners who join themselves to the Lord, to minister to Him, and to love the name of the Lord, to be His servants, every one who keeps from profaning the sabbath and holds fast to My covenant; even those I will bring to My holy mountain and make them joyful in My house of prayer. Their burnt offerings and their sacrifices will be acceptable on My altar; for My house will be called a house of prayer for all the peoples" (Isaiah 56:6–7).

It's difficult to believe that Ruth would have made that drastic switch from pagan gods to the one true God if Naomi's faith had not somehow shone through the gloom of her grief. The glimpses of God Naomi revealed through the hardships of life were evidently powerful enough to make Ruth want to follow Naomi and, by extension, her God. Even the darkest times in our lives can create a backdrop that magnifies a glimmer of faith-light before a watching world. Ruth had witnessed Naomi at her worst, gripped in the throes of crushing grief and yet, she had also observed Naomi's faith in her God. The very act of crying out to God, even questioning His actions toward us, carries an implied acknowledgement of His existence and involvement in our lives, even when we don't understand His ways.

Despite rough terrain and potential perils along the way, the two unaccompanied widows arrived safely in Bethlehem, proof of God's loving watch-care over them. "And when they had come to Bethlehem, all the city was stirred because of them, and the women said, 'Is this Naomi?'" (Ruth 1:19). We can imagine Naomi's old friends doing a double take when they glimpsed her sorrow-ravaged, grief-worn face. Naomi said to them, "Do not call me Naomi [*sweetness*]; call me Mara [*bitter*] for the Almighty has dealt very bitterly with me" (Ruth 1:20).

Naomi's return to Bethlehem roused the curiosity of the entire city. The last imprinted image in their minds was of a younger Naomi, married to Elimelech, mothering two young sons. Whenever we run into someone we haven't seen in a while who has undergone drastic change, we need to adjust the mental picture of them stored in our brains. One of my relatives underwent facial plastic surgery and I walked right by her in a hospital corridor. She had to call out my name before I belatedly recognized her.

How difficult it must have been for Naomi to return to her hometown, see her old house, visit her favorite shops, and renew friendships, all without the context of husband and children. Bittersweet memories must have assaulted her each time she recalled past experiences in Bethlehem as it related to her family's enjoyment of them. She couldn't point to a familiar landmark and say to her husband or sons, "Remember when . . .?" I often refer to my husband, Mark, as "keeper-of-the-memories and taker-of-the-pictures" for our family. I rely heavily on his phenomenal memory for places, dates, details, and experiences.

The word Naomi used for God the Almighty is *Shaddai*. By using this name for God, Naomi acknowledged His sovereignty and His all-sufficiency.[20] Complaining about His treatment of her in permitting her husband and sons to die did not negate her belief in Him. On the contrary, it confirmed her belief that His actions could not be thwarted. He is all powerful and in complete control of our lives. If His fingerprints are all over the joys in our lives, then they must be over our sorrows as well. He is either God Almighty, the Sovereign One, or He's not.

But whenever we allow our grief to dictate our theology, instead of the other way around, we can sometimes unknowingly present a picture of weakened faith to a watching world. "On the one hand, she [Naomi] had responded to the report of Yahweh's favor upon Bethlehem by setting out for home (v. 6), and then wishing upon her daughters-in-law the blessing of Yahweh the God of Israel (vv. 8–9).

On the other hand, she seems to have conceded to pagan world-views by acknowledging that Orpah had returned to her gods (v. 15). Naomi may have come back home in faith, but hers is a flawed faith. Unable to see human causation in Israel's famine and in her own trials, the woman the neighbors greet is a bitter old woman. She does indeed ascribe sovereignty to God, but this is a sovereignty without grace, an omnipotent power without compassion, a judicial will without mercy."[21]

Naomi then explained to the women that she had left Bethlehem full but had returned empty (Ruth 1:21). In fairness, Naomi did not leave Bethlehem completely full; she left hungry, starving, and desperate to flee the famine. She did leave full in the sense of her family being intact when they departed. Nor did Naomi return completely empty. She had a devoted daughter-in-law by her side, pledged to remain with her through thick and thin. Surrounded by sympathetic friends, Naomi's barely healed wounds gushed open and bitterness flooded her soul as she rehearsed her compounded grief. Naomi was only human. Revisiting past pain can sweep us away in its undertow and we can lose our emotional footing, forgetting our present blessings. Ruth was certainly a blessing that Naomi would only come to fully realize in the insecure days ahead.

As God orchestrated it, the two women arrived at the beginning of barley harvest (Ruth 1:22). "Now Naomi had a kinsman of her husband, a man of great wealth, of the family of Elimelech, whose name was Boaz" (Ruth 2:1). In the tribal system under which Israel operated, blood relatives were assigned a specific hierarchy inherent with certain obligations. Naomi had returned to Bethlehem husbandless and childless. Her closest blood relative, therefore, would have been put on notice that he needed to step in and help Elimelech's and Mahlon's names live on through offspring (Deuteronomy 25:5–10).

In marrying Elimelech, Naomi would have known about all his relatives, including exactly how closely or distantly they were related. So of course, she knew about Boaz, one of Elimelech's blood relatives. Even through famine, Boaz had managed to hang on to his property and enjoyed reaping the fruit of all his hard work. He owned productive fields and employed numerous workers to harvest his barley and other crops. The name Boaz means *swift strength.*[22]

In Naomi's day, barley was widely cultivated as the main food source for the poor. Depending on the rainy season, barley could be planted around December and then harvested in late spring. The grain was easy to plant because it could be sown on soil that didn't need plowing. This fact enabled farmers to grow barley on small plots of land inaccessible to draft animals. Barley is still an important food crop near Bethlehem today. The small plots of barley are harvested by hand as described in the book of Ruth, a book with many references to barley. The peasant women cut the grain, and then tie them into bundles to dry. When dry, the barley is taken by donkey to the threshing floors to be threshed using modern equipment, or with an old-fashioned threshing sledge pulled by an animal.[23]

With Ruth now a permanent part of her family, Naomi introduced her to family members and friends. As a destitute widow returning to Bethlehem, Naomi did have some land that had belonged to her late husband (Ruth 4:3). Ordinarily, land passed from father to son because it was important to keep property in the family down through the generations. If a man had no sons, he could legally bestow his land to his daughter or daughters, as in the case of Zelophehad's five daughters (Numbers 27). There was no law for a husband passing land on to his wife. Naomi may have had Elimelech's land in her "portfolio," but in her impoverished condition, could do nothing with it. The two widows needed to eat, and Ruth was willing to work. "And Ruth the Moabitess said to Naomi, 'Please let me go to the field and glean among the ears of grain after one in whose sight I may find favor.' And she said to her, 'Go, my daughter'" (Ruth 2:2). Ruth wanted to find a reaper who would allow her to follow behind to collect the bits and pieces of grain dropped along the way.

Naomi knew that many landowners adhered to God's law as stated in Leviticus 19:9, "When you harvest the crops of your land, do not harvest the grain along the edges of your fields, and do not pick up what the harvesters drop" (NLT). In Deuteronomy 24:19, God promised to bless the landowners for obeying this law, "When you are harvesting your crops and forget to bring in a bundle of grain from your field, don't go back to get it. Leave it for the foreigners, orphans, and widows. Then the Lord your God will bless you in all you do" (NLT). As a foreigner and widow, Ruth certainly qualified as one who deserved to gather the permissible leftovers.

Ruth just "happened" to choose a field belonging to Naomi's relative, Boaz. Of course, as the story unfolds, we see God's gracious governance over every aspect of these two widows' lives. When Boaz spied this strange woman among his normal reapers, his curiosity was aroused. The servant in charge of the reapers informed him that Ruth, a young Moabite woman, had returned with Naomi. The servant, observing Ruth's industrious work, reported her diligence to Boaz. Drawn to her, Boaz said to Ruth, "Listen carefully, my daughter. Do not go to glean in another field; furthermore, do not go on from this one, but stay here with my maids. Let your eyes be on the field which they reap, and go after them. Indeed, I have commanded the servants not to touch you. When you are thirsty, go to the water jars and drink from what the servants draw" (Ruth 2:8–9). As an older man showing care and concern for a young widow, Boaz called her "my daughter," just as Naomi did. His fatherly advice touched

Ruth deeply, even as she questioned it as a foreigner from Moab. But Boaz assured her that the story of all she had done for Naomi, and all she had left behind, had been fully reported to him. Boaz prayed a blessing over Ruth and beseeched God to reward her work and make her wages full because she had sought refuge under God's wings (Ruth 2:10–12). There is no more secure place for the believer than under God's divine protection, and Boaz desired that for Ruth.

Increasingly attracted to Ruth, Boaz singled her out to share a meal with him. He dished out so much food in front of her that she had plenty of leftovers to take home to Naomi. He even gave further instructions to his workers to not bother her in any way, or make her feel uncomfortable. In fact, Boaz went beyond the provision of the law to tell his gleaners to purposely pull grain from their bundles and leave it on the ground behind them for Ruth to gather (Ruth 2:13–16). Imagine how protected and secure Ruth felt, working with gleaners who treated her with generosity and respect.

Mark and I met at a church in Phoenix, Arizona, two days after I had arrived from Argentina. I was sixteen and ready to begin my senior year of high school in the States. We had our first date just days after our youth pastor introduced us to each other. As I made new friends in the youth group, I began to wonder why none of the other boys expressed any interest in me, or asked me out on a date. I eventually found out why. Mark had gathered all the guys together to tell them "Hands off, she's mine!" As an eighteen-year-old, Mark enjoyed a little authority over the guys my age, and they listened to him. Through extraordinary measures and elaborate instructions, Boaz was telling his guys, "Hands off, she's mine!"

Ruth labored hard all day, bent over in the hot sun, gathering every scrap she could. When she beat out all she had gleaned, separating the grain from the chaff, it came to about half a bushel, or thirty pounds of barley (Ruth 2:17). This would have filled their bare pantry and provided something to trade for produce and meat. As Ruth trudged home carrying her precious load of grain, Naomi waited anxiously to hear how God had provided for her devoted daughter-in-law. Upon arriving home, the first thing Ruth did was pull out her packet of leftovers from lunch and give them to Naomi, who ate until she was satisfied (Ruth 2:18). Ruth gleaned enough barley on her first day of work to "sustain the two women for about five days."[24] Given the duration of the harvest season and Ruth's continued reaping, she and Naomi would have had enough food to last them for a year.

Curious, Naomi asked, "Where did you glean today and where did you work? May he who took notice of you be blessed" (Ruth 2:19). Naomi knew Ruth's payload did not fit the norm for a poor stranger gathering a few stalks from the corners of a field. Naomi spontaneously proclaimed a blessing on this kind landowner. How Naomi's heart must have stirred within her when Ruth replied, "The name of the man with whom I worked today is Boaz" (Ruth 2:19). Again, Naomi asked God to bless this relative. She also acknowledged the Lord's hand in this marvelous turn of events (Ruth 2:20). Earlier Naomi had complained to her friends in Bethlehem that the Lord had dealt bitterly with her. She asked them to call her Mara instead of Naomi because she believed her lot in life would be one of continual suffering. Yet now, Naomi had to publicly admit that the Lord had not withdrawn His kindness, *hesed*, from her. Perhaps she regretted her request to be called *Bitter*, now that her life was starting to become *Pleasant* once more.

Naomi had fully incorporated her daughter-in-law into her life, and into her family, as evidenced by her next words to Ruth, "This man is our relative, he is one of our closest relatives" (Ruth 2:20). Naomi didn't say "my," she said "our." Boaz was as much Ruth's relative as he was Naomi's. When Ruth relayed Boaz's extravagant offer of allowing her to restrict her gleaning specifically to his fields, under his watchful eye, Naomi recognized His proffered kindness as the ultimate protection from unscrupulous workers who might have taken unfair advantage of her status as a lowly female foreigner (Ruth 2:21–22). Respectful of Naomi's wishes and grateful for Boaz's protection, Ruth gleaned until the end of barley harvest and stayed on to harvest wheat through part of the summer (Ruth 2:23). How Naomi must have admired and appreciated Ruth's dedicated devotion to her as she saw Ruth out the door every morning and welcomed her back each evening. Naomi had food on the table and a measure of security for the future thanks to Ruth's hard labor.

One fateful day, near the end of harvesting, Naomi said to Ruth, "My daughter, shall I not seek security for you, that it may be well with you?" (Ruth 3:1). Naomi enjoyed security thanks to Ruth's industriousness, and she saw a way to secure Ruth's future, and her own, in a bold matchmaking venture. So she asked Ruth, "Now is not Boaz our kinsman, with whose maids you were?" (Ruth 3:2). In the Old Testament social structure, the nearest kinsman-redeemer had three responsibilities: He had the right to recover forfeited property of a kinsman (Leviticus 25:25), he had the obligation to purchase the freedom of one who had fallen into slavery (Leviticus 25:47–49), and if he was a brother-in-law, he was required to marry the widow of his closest male relative to provide an heir to continue the name of the deceased (Deuteronomy 25:5–10).[25]

Boaz was not the closest kinsman, nor did he fall within the parameters of Deuteronomy 25 as a brother-in-law, required to fulfill the duties of a levirate. Technically not bound to fulfill the obligations listed in the law, Boaz responded out of grace and mercy to the two disenfranchised widows. Naomi would have carefully noted

Boaz's evident partiality to Ruth, surmising that since he obviously felt some affection for her, he might be persuaded to step into the role of kinsman-redeemer based on love, not just duty. "Behold, he winnows barley at the threshing floor tonight" (Ruth 3:2). Obviously, Ruth, a worker in Boaz's fields, would have known about the important upcoming threshing event, a big deal in those days, celebrating a bountiful harvest. The people of Bethlehem took turns using the communal threshing floor, a slightly raised platform with a flat, hard surface. In threshing, the grain was beaten out from the stalks with flails, or trodden by oxen. In winnowing, the grain was thrown into the air so the wind could blow the chaff away. The grain was then removed from the threshing floor and placed in heaps to be sold or stored in granaries.[26] The threshing floor was usually located outside town in a place where the prevailing west wind could be used to full advantage.[27]

Naomi's next words may have shocked Ruth to the core. Knowing that Boaz, the landowner, would assuredly be at the threshing floor on such an important night, Naomi said to her daughter-in-law, "So bathe yourself, rub on some perfumed oil, and get dressed up. Then go down to the threshing floor. But don't let the man know you're there until he finishes his meal. When he gets ready to go to sleep, take careful notice of the place where he lies down. Then go, uncover his legs, and lie down beside him. He will tell you what you should do" (Ruth 3:3–4, NET).

Naomi wanted Ruth to make herself as attractive as possible, but remain hidden until it was the right time to reveal herself to Boaz. Ruth cloaked herself with an outer garment, serving to keep her well hidden from Boaz while he was supervising the threshing and then celebrating with eating and drinking.[28] Since Ruth planned to spend the night in a field, she would have gladly welcomed this outer covering, or blanket, to help ward off the chilly night air.[29] Naomi wanted Ruth to remain out of sight, yet keep a vigilant eye on Boaz, noticing exactly when and where he lay down on the threshing floor. Naomi's explicit instructions called for great courage from Ruth, a widowed foreigner. Putting ourselves in her difficult situation that night, we can imagine that Ruth waited quietly in the dark, until everyone around Boaz slept soundly, before she carried out Naomi's daring and calculated plan. The less witnesses to her bold act, the better!

Some translations read that Ruth uncovered Boaz's feet; others say legs. However, legs, or lower body, may be a better translation than feet. Because *foot* is sometimes used euphemistically for the genitals, some feel that Ruth uncovered more than just Boaz's feet, uncovering his legs as well. While Ruth and Boaz did not actually have a sexual encounter at the threshing floor, there is no doubt that Ruth's actions were symbolic and constituted a marriage proposal.[30]

Once Ruth uncovered Boaz's legs, she was to lie down beside him. Then, she was to wait to see what Boaz would say. With fast-beating heart, and trembling hands, Ruth faithfully carried out all of Naomi's detailed instructions because she had promised her mother-in-law, "I will do everything you have told me to do" (Ruth 3:5, NET). The fact that Ruth agreed to follow through on everything Naomi told her, emphasizes the closeness and respect Ruth had for her mother-in-law. She may not have fully understood all the implications inherent in Naomi's request, but she trusted her mother-in-law enough to obey her to the letter, even for an uncertain outcome. Neither woman could predict exactly what Boaz would say, or how he would react to Ruth's seemingly brazen maneuvers, although surely Naomi hoped her daughter-in-law's actions would engender a favorable response.

"So she went down to the threshing floor and did according to all that her mother-in-law had commanded her" (Ruth 3:6).

"When Boaz had finished his meal and was feeling satisfied, he lay down to sleep at the far end of the grain heap. Then Ruth crept up quietly, uncovered his legs, and lay down beside him. In the middle of the night he was startled and turned over. Now he saw a woman lying beside him! He said, 'Who are you?' She replied, 'I am Ruth, your servant'" (Ruth 3:7–9, NET).

Have you noticed how men can be more approachable when their stomachs are full? An old proverb says, "The way to a man's heart is through his stomach." A Jamaican proverb says it a little differently, "You can say anything to a man with a full stomach." Yet another wrote, "I defy you to agitate any fellow with a full stomach."[31] Boaz had a merry heart and a full stomach from celebrating a successful harvest. His position at the far end of the grain heap automatically made his proximity a deterrent to would-be thieves. Something startled Boaz awake in the middle of the night, perhaps his uncovered legs growing cold. When he turned over, presumably to cover his exposed lower extremities, he discovered Ruth lying beside him in the dark.

He may have smelled her before he saw her. Surrounded by threshers reeking of sharp, salty sweat, the aroma of Ruth's sweet perfume would have seemed entirely out of context. Ruth was the only one on the threshing floor, and surrounding areas that evening, who had not put in a hard day's work. Perhaps he had never smelled such a sweet smell on the threshing floor! Maybe that's why he knew it must be a woman lying next to him. Without adequate light however, he couldn't see which woman shared his space. When Boaz asked her identity, she replied, "I am Ruth, your servant." In Ruth's first interchange with Boaz, she had referred to herself as a humble menial servant, using the Hebrew word *shifkhah* (Ruth 2:13). But in this conversation with Boaz, Ruth elevated her servant-status to *amah,* a higher class of servant, perhaps in preparation for her proposal to Boaz.[32]

Once Boaz awakened to discover Ruth, she didn't wait for him to tell her what to do. In that regard, she improvised on Naomi's prior orders to her. Maybe Ruth sensed the need to seize the moment and maintain the momentum of surprise. Certainly, God used her next words to Boaz; "So spread your covering over your maid, for you are a close relative" (Ruth 3:9). As one writer clarified, Naomi wanted Ruth to remove the blanket or cloak that covered Boaz's legs and feet while he slept on the threshing floor. Then Naomi wanted Ruth to ask Boaz to cover her with his blanket. This was a symbolic way of requesting Boaz's protection as her husband.[33]

Ruth's request to Boaz contained a wonderful word play in the Hebrew language. Earlier, when Ruth first met Boaz, he had expressed the hope that she would find sustenance and shelter underneath the "wings" *kanaph* of God. When Boaz awoke, startled to find Ruth positioned at his feet, she reused his own poetic language to imply that in the act of covering her, or spreading his wings over her, he would fulfill her hope for sustenance and shelter.[34] This word, *kanaph,* can refer not only to the wings of a bird, but also to a covering, the corners of one's flowing garments. To "spread one's wings over someone" was a euphemistic idiom for marriage. Boaz, an astute man, quickly interpreted Ruth's request not as a demand for sex, but as a proposition for marriage.[35] Had Naomi been there that night, I believe she would have been so proud of her daughter-in-law. By faith, Ruth had wholeheartedly embraced Naomi's God and Israel's system of a kinsman-redeemer. Acting in faith, Ruth risked ridicule, rejection, and even loss of future work if Boaz responded negatively to her loaded request.

We can imagine Naomi not getting much sleep that night as she beseeched God's favor and blessing on Ruth's brave mission. Boaz's response to Naomi's plan, as carried out by Ruth, could determine the future of these two widows. Thankfully, Boaz responded positively when he answered Ruth's plea for his protection and financial support, "May you be blessed of the Lord, my daughter. You have shown your last kindness to be better than the first by not going after young men, whether poor or rich" (Ruth 3:10). Boaz was obviously interested in Ruth, but perhaps assumed she would rather marry a man nearer her age. In calling Ruth his "daughter," Boaz placed himself in a fatherly category that promised respect and proper treatment of this young widow. This was a man who could be trusted to not take advantage of Ruth's vulnerable position on the threshing floor.

Boaz acknowledged Ruth's first kindness, or act of devotion, as "her decision to remain and help Naomi. The latter act of devotion was her decision to marry Boaz to provide a child to carry on her deceased husband's (and Elimelech's) line and to provide for Naomi in her old age."[36] How kind of Boaz to sense the courage it took for Ruth to enact Naomi's plan! Perhaps he noticed the toll it took emotionally because he said to her, "Now, my daughter, do not fear. I will do for you whatever you ask, for all my people in the city know that you are a woman of excellence" (Ruth 3:11). Perhaps Ruth had been called many names living in Israel: words like *stranger, foreigner, Moabitess, widow, poor*, or *Naomi's daughter*. To be called a woman of excellence, based on her kind and loyal treatment of Naomi, must have warmed her heart on that chilly night. The Hebrew word for "excellence," *hayil*, is the same one used for the virtuous woman depicted in Proverbs 31.[37] "Boaz's description of Ruth as a woman of "excellence" (NASB) or "noble character" (NIV, Heb. *hayil*) is interesting because the same Hebrew word describes Boaz in 2:1. *Hayil* means a person of wealth, character, virtue, attainment, and comprehensive excellence. As such Ruth was worthy to be the wife of Boaz. They were two of a kind."[38]

We can just imagine the intense relief that flooded Ruth the moment she knew the plan had succeeded and she heard Boaz's encouraging words. Naomi was indeed blessed with this daughter-in-law whose excellent character and stellar reputation had enhanced their standing in Bethlehem. Boaz, a man of the highest integrity, had to let Ruth know one vital detail, "Now it is true I am a close relative; however, there is a relative closer than I" (Ruth 3:12). We may wonder, had we heard those words, if we would have immediately thought, "Oh no, this entire nerve-racking night has been in vain!" Perhaps Ruth questioned if Naomi had made a terrible mistake and targeted the wrong kinsman-redeemer. Boaz's next words probably stirred up Ruth's swirling emotions even higher, "Remain this night, and when morning comes, if he will redeem you, good; let him redeem you. But if he does not wish to redeem you, then I will redeem you, as the Lord lives. Lie down until morning" (Ruth 3:13). Boaz displayed honor and integrity in choosing to follow correct protocol according to their custom and the law of the levirate. His words are even more impressive if he indeed had feelings for Ruth and wanted her for himself. If so, his altruistic virtue is admirable.

Naomi must have known that her unusual and difficult instructions would have made sleep almost impossible for her dear daughter-in-law. After their hushed exchange, Boaz told Ruth to lie down until morning. It would be difficult, if not impossible, to sleep with that much uncertainty looming over her. Ruth probably wished she could speak with Naomi right then and there, desiring her wisdom and further directions about what to do. It must have been very reassuring, however, to hear Boaz invoke the Lord's name in his promise to redeem her if the other man did not. This showed how seriously he took his commitment to her.

"So she lay at his feet until morning and rose before one could recognize another; and he said, 'Let it not be known that the woman came to the threshing floor'" (Ruth 3:14). Boaz wanted to preserve Ruth's sterling reputation, and his own as well. No need to add any fuel to the town gossips' fire! Grouped with others on the threshing floor, their entire exchange took place in whispers, or very low murmurs, close to each other's ears. Fortunately, they could keep their dialogue private.

Before Boaz dismissed Ruth, he wanted to bless her even more so he said, "'Give me the cloak that is on you and hold it.' So she held it, and he measured six measures of barley and laid it on her. Then she went into the city" (Ruth 3:15). Close to the huge pile of threshed grain, Boaz could easily ladle out six measures of barley into her cloak. "The 'measure' was probably the seah (one-third of an ephah or about ten pounds). Thus, six seahs would equal about sixty pounds. Ruth was a strong woman able to carry such a heavy load. Probably Boaz placed the burden on her head."[39]

We can imagine Naomi anxiously awaiting Ruth's return. It's quite likely she didn't sleep much that night either, as she nervously wondered about all the events transpiring. Perhaps she entertained a heavy heart as she imagined all that could go wrong with her presumptuous plan. When at last, Ruth entered their home, Naomi eagerly inquired, "'How did it go, my daughter?' And she told her all that the man had done for her" (Ruth 3:16). Naomi would have wanted to hear every single detail. Certainly, the women went over all that had transpired several times, dissecting the conversation between Boaz and Ruth, and marveling at how the Lord had guided Ruth's every step. Perhaps Naomi praised Ruth's departure from the original script when she heard how the clandestine encounter played out. When it comes to tales of romance and intrigue, women are prone to say, "Tell me everything! Don't leave out a single detail!" We can derive a vicarious thrill from another's retelling of their love story.

We may wonder why Naomi tried to set Ruth up with Boaz. Surely, she must have known Elimelech had a nearer kinsman. In her day, that was not something you would overlook or feign ignorance about. We can only ask some "I wonder" questions as we interact with the text. For example: Had Naomi already scoped out the other man and deduced that he would be unwilling or unable to marry Ruth? Did Naomi bank on Boaz's honorable integrity to sort out the matter and do the right thing? In this male-driven society, did Naomi hope Boaz would solidify what she could not by making sure Ruth's future was secure—either with him or with the other man?

After Ruth recounted her story, she revealed the treasure wrapped up in her cloak. She told Naomi, "These six measures of barley he gave to me, for he said, 'Do not go to your mother-in-law empty-handed'" (Ruth 3:17). This generous bounty of grain further proved Boaz's interest in Ruth and his respect for Naomi; a sweet promise of future security for the women. Perhaps he guessed correctly that Naomi was behind all that had transpired that night, and this spontaneous generosity conveyed his gratitude.

Naomi had additional wisdom to impart. She instructed Ruth, "Wait, my daughter, until you know how the matter turns out; for the man will not rest until he has settled it today" (Ruth 3:18). Naomi's resiliency in the face of adversity is to be commended. Her multiple tragedies may have prematurely aged her, but her spirit remained indomitable, and her sharp mind granted her keen insight. Naomi may have been a poor, disenfranchised widow, but she accomplished amazing things by responding astutely to people and circumstances with impeccable timing.

True to Naomi's prediction, Boaz headed straight for the gates of the city, where all the important business was conducted, and sat down to wait for the closer relative to pass by. Boaz pulled his friend aside, gathered ten town elders as witnesses, and informed him that Naomi had returned from the land of Moab and needed to sell the piece of land belonging to Elimelech. At first, the closer relative told Boaz he would be willing to redeem the land, but when he learned that acquiring Ruth the Moabitess would be a nonnegotiable part of the deal, he backpedaled, claiming the arrangement would jeopardize his own inheritance (Ruth 4:1–6). By marrying Ruth, the firstborn son he had with her would be considered Mahlon's legal heir and the land would eventually pass on to him. Perhaps the closer relative felt the drain on his own finances would not be worth the duty of keeping the land in Elimelech's name. Maybe he feared his own children's inheritance would be shortchanged. Also in play, could have been the fact that Ruth was a Moabitess. As a foreigner, albeit one who had embraced Israel's God, the idea of marrying Ruth may have been off-putting to him.

In Naomi's day, "A man would remove his sandal and give it to the other party. This was a legally binding act in Israel" (Ruth 4:7, NET). In front of all the witnesses, the closer relative removed his sandal and handed it over to Boaz. This "symbolized Boaz's right to walk on the land as his property."[40] Boaz told the witnesses that he had officially purchased all Elimelech's land and with it, Ruth's hand in marriage. They unanimously confirmed the transaction and added their blessing, asking God to bless Ruth with fertility and Boaz with wealth and honor (Ruth 4:9–12).

Boaz, himself, was the product of a mixed marriage. His mother, Rahab, a Canaanite prostitute, had converted to Judaism and married a devout Jew named Salmon (Matthew 1:5). Perhaps his own heritage made him sensitive to Ruth's plight and more than willing to join his life with hers. By the time Boaz, an older man, and Ruth married, Rahab most likely had departed this earth, but it's interesting to know these two women were related by marriage!

The Lord answered the prayer of the witnesses, and no doubt Naomi's prayer as well, because God enabled Ruth to conceive and give birth to a son. How Naomi must have rejoiced at this wonderful turn of events. We can picture her lovingly coddling Ruth during her pregnancy, and weeping tears of joy at the birth of her grandson. Quite a contrast to Naomi's earlier bitter tears! We can imagine how jubilantly the women welcomed this baby boy into their lives as they celebrated the security he represented. Ruth had remained barren during her ten-year marriage to Mahlon, and perhaps Naomi worried that she might continue that way in her marriage to Boaz.

The women of Bethlehem rallied around Naomi and crowned her with uplifting words, "Blessed is the Lord who has not left you without a redeemer today, and may his name become famous in Israel" (Ruth 4:14). Even though scholars are divided on whether it's Boaz or Obed who imbues the role of kinsman-redeemer for Ruth, the main issue is the assurance that with the birth of this little boy, the women's future would be secured. Boaz would set the standard for tender care and Obed could be counted upon to carry on his legacy as Boaz aged and died. Hope for a bright future resided in the life of this tiny child.

Naomi had lost both her boys, but because of Ruth's beautiful display of *hesed*, the women of Bethlehem clearly recognized the invaluable asset Ruth had become in Naomi's life. In fact, they reminded Naomi that her daughter-in-law, who loved her, was better to her than seven sons (Ruth 4:15). "Then Naomi took the child and laid him in her lap, and became his nurse" (Ruth 4:16). With this wonderful turn of events, Naomi's bitter heart could be transformed into one of tender gratitude. Those of us who enjoy grandchildren know the thrill of welcoming them into this world. We may echo the sentiment that had we known grandchildren could be so much fun, we would have had them first! According to the text, Boaz and Ruth did not name their son; Naomi's friends did. "The neighbor women gave him a name, saying, 'A son has been born to Naomi!' So they named him Obed [*servant*].[41] He is the father of Jesse, the father of David" (Ruth 4:17).

We could almost add "and they lived happily ever after" to this story that began so tragically and ended so triumphantly. Two women who had no sure recourse in their widowhood found security. Two women who faced an uncertain and frightening future found hope. Two women who lost loved ones found ones to love again. Two women who craved kindness found it. Two women who were pitied by all who knew them found renewed esteem in the eyes of others—all because God provided a kinsman-redeemer for them.

Believers can appreciate all the parallels to our own lives when we recognize that Jesus Christ is our Redeemer. Just as Boaz had to be related, willing, and able to redeem Ruth, our Savior is related as the God-Man, and He is willing and able to redeem us for all eternity. I'm so grateful that our God is in the business of renewing all He redeems and giving us bright hope for the future! When we remember the utter depravity of our lost state, we can better appreciate the eternal difference He has made in our lives. We can believe that Naomi and Ruth expressed continual gratitude to God for their deliverance each time they recalled the former despair over their desperate circumstances.

In engaging with Naomi's story, several recurring themes come to the forefront: loyalty, security, and love. As we develop these in the application points below, noting how they related to Naomi's life and recognizing how they relate to ours, may we appreciate the dramatic difference our Redeemer makes in our lives as we follow our Leader, find our security, and fathom His *hesed*.

Follow our Leader

Every main character in Naomi's story followed someone. We express our loyalty by choosing someone to follow. Ruth's wholehearted loyalty to Naomi is a prime example (Ruth 1:16–17). Her vow, "though obviously not marital in nature, is often included in modern wedding ceremonies to communicate the depths of devotion to which new couples aspire."[42] Obviously, Ruth's loyalty to Naomi was motivated by her decision to follow God.

When we make Jesus our leader and choose to follow Him, He blesses our loyalty. Psalm 23:1–3 explains that when we follow our Shepherd, we will want for nothing because He will lead us to lush, green pastures and quiet, refreshing waters. He will never lead us astray because He is the perfect Leader. As He leads us through this life, He will revive our soul and continually renew our strength. As our all-sufficient leader, God provides His Spirit to comfort us, and

His Word to feed us. All His paths are righteous ones so we can be confident that when we follow Him, we are doing what most benefits us and best pleases Him.

I have battled a fear of being completely submerged in water due to a near-drowning experience in the Pacific Ocean at a young age. I especially dislike the sensation of water flooding into my eyes and ears. Before Mark and I married, he once tried to help me overcome this fear. One afternoon, while enjoying a friend's apartment complex pool, Mark was happily diving into the deep end, and I was peacefully standing safely knee-high in the shallow end with all the little children, when Mark persuaded me to venture into the deep end with him. Holding his hand in a death-grip vise, we descended the pool's slope into deeper waters. I panicked the instant water reached my neck. Somehow, I lost my footing, let go of Mark's hand, and began flailing about, scared to death. Mark, in full adrenalin mode, grabbed my waist and hoisted me above his head, keeping his own submerged, as he practically ran toward the shallow end. He didn't put me down until we reached the edge of the pool. I remember feeling so foolish for having put on such a display, but I also marveled at my man's swift strength. His quick actions helped solidify my loyalty to him that day.

Naomi and Ruth may not have been panicking in a pool, but they were drowning in the eyes of society due to their many misfortunes. Boaz, whose name means *swift strength*, came to their rescue in dramatic ways. His actions, fueled by his godly character, earned the loyalty and trust of both impoverished women. When we were drowning in our sin, hopeless and helpless, God sent Jesus to rescue us with His atoning death on the cross. He is supremely worthy of our loyalty and trust now, and throughout eternity.

Find our Security

We women place a high value on security and often struggle to maintain emotional equilibrium whenever we feel insecure. When basic needs are threatened, we can succumb to fear just as Naomi did. When loved ones upon whom we depend suddenly leave our lives, debilitating grief can cripple us, violently shaking our sense of security, and making us bitter like Naomi was for a time.

Psalm 23:4–5 is a beautiful picture of the security God provides. Even when we walk through the valley of the shadow of death, He is with us. Even when bad things happen in our lives, He is with us. "Your rod and Your staff, they comfort me" (Psalm 23:4b). "A shepherd uses his implements to assure the sheep of his presence and calm their nerves. The underlying reality is the emotional stability God provides during life-threatening situations."[43] Even when we feel assaulted by unrelenting adversity, we can still find refuge in Him. Even when circumstances threaten to drain us dry, we can receive full satisfaction and bountiful refreshment from His presence. Even when we are so confused we don't know which way to turn, we can find all the direction we need in His Word.

Living in north Texas has given me a healthy respect for tornado season, where we often find ourselves under tornado watches or warnings. One late afternoon in spring, Mark, our youngest son Jeremy, and I, were home when we noticed the sky darkening. We turned on the news to hear of a tornado possibly headed our way. As the winds increased and our power went out, the three of us, including our dog, huddled inside the bathtub of an interior bathroom. We heard what sounded like the roar of a freight train and knew the twister had to be close. Jeremy, home from college on spring break said, "I love you guys," as we prepared to get hit. Thankfully, the tornado veered away from our house at the last moment and we were spared. Sadly, other homes and businesses around us were not. At that moment, our temporary security rested in interior walls and a bathtub. Thankfully, as believers, our permanent security is grounded in our God and in His perfect will for us.

Rehearsing God's attributes helps reinforce our belief in Him and attests to His authenticity before others. We find our security in Him when we choose to put into practice what we believe about Him based on His Word. Naomi found her security in the belief that God alone provides food (Ruth 1:6), bestows *hesed* (1:8), grants security (1:9), and is sovereign (1:13, 21). Ruth found her security in the belief that God is omniscient and judges righteously (1:17). Boaz found his security in the belief that God bestows His presence and blessings on people (2:4), rewards work with full wages (2:12), provides refuge for those who seek it (2:12), and blesses those who show kindness to others (3:10). The elders of Bethlehem found their security in the belief that God oversees fertility and prosperity (4:11–12). Naomi's friends found their security in the belief that God enabled Ruth to conceive and bear a son, representing security for Naomi (4:14).

Fathom His Hesed

"Fathom" means to *measure* or *to understand something complicated or mysterious.* I don't think we will fully fathom God's loyal love and unfailing lovingkindness for us until we get to heaven. In fact, God tells us that He will spend eternity demonstrating "the surpassing wealth of his grace in kindness toward us in Christ Jesus" (Ephesians 2:7, NET). One of my favorite stanzas from an old poem states, "When I stand before the throne, dressed in beauty not my own, when I see Thee as Thou art, love Thee with unsinning heart, then, Lord shall I fully know—not till then—how much I owe."[44] While we may never plumb all the depths, nor ever fully comprehend the limitlessness of God's *hesed* for us in this life, I believe He delights in watching us test and prove His loyal love for us in every circumstance we encounter as we dare to fathom the depths of His *hesed*.

God's *hesed* is all over Naomi's story. Ruth pledged to follow Naomi and her God; perhaps without fully understanding that, in doing so, God's *hesed* would be following her all the days of her life. Psalm 23:6 promises, "Surely goodness and lovingkindness [*hesed*] will follow me all the days of my life, and I will dwell in the house of the Lord forever." Naomi followed God's leading back to Bethlehem, perhaps without fully fathoming that God's *hesed* was following her. Boaz followed through with his commitment to fulfill his duty as a kinsman-redeemer, perhaps without fully comprehending that God's *hesed* was following his every step and, through him, spilling over into the lives of Naomi and Ruth.

Before undergoing a complete hysterectomy, I used to suffer from a series of large ovarian cysts that would rupture and then require emergency surgery. My first surgery for this condition took place at age thirteen. A few years later, Mark (nineteen) and I (seventeen) had just worked up the courage to say the "I love you" words to each other when another cyst presented itself in the form of intense pain. I feared another surgery might be necessary. It was. Lying in my hospital bed, looking terrible, and feeling nauseous after my surgery, Mark walked in unannounced to visit me. As we conversed, I started gagging, trying to hold back the inevitable. Mark, assessing the situation, rushed to grab the ubiquitous pink throw-up basin every hospital room in America uses in its decor. He positioned it under my chin and held it there while I proceeded to fill it up. Talk about humiliating! He had never seen me look anything but my best as I dressed up for our dates. Now he saw me clothed in the most unflattering garment ever made, hair disheveled, vomiting all over myself! I wondered if he would still love me after this disgusting display. Amazingly, he told me he loved me right after he emptied the pink basin into the toilet, and I believed him. That degrading experience helped me fathom the depths of his love for me.

As we navigate the unexpected twists and turns that define life here on earth, each one is an opportunity to fathom God's *hesed* for us. Just like Naomi, Ruth, and Boaz tasted God's lovingkindness in their lives, so can we. Psalm 34:8–9 exhorts us to, "Taste and see that the Lord is good! How blessed is the one who takes shelter in him! Remain loyal to the Lord, you chosen people of his, for his loyal followers lack nothing!" (NET).

In our pressure-cooker lives, it's sometimes easy to forget how completely, permanently, and constantly our God loves us. Our fickle hearts and frazzled minds need frequent reminders because, just like a tossing boat, we can be easily swayed by the external distractions and internal doubts comprising this life on earth. One way to be reminded of God's everlasting lovingkindness for us is to wear a piece of jewelry with the word "love" on it, or just a simple heart. This tangible reminder of His intangible *hesed* can serve to encourage our needy hearts. As believers in Jesus, we are invited to follow our Leader, find all our security in Him, and fathom the depths of His love for us. It's the adventure of a lifetime!

Father God, how grateful we are that You didn't give up on Naomi when all the traumas of her life caused her to doubt You. Lord, even when our faith wavers and we question Your sovereignty, You remain absolutely faithful and continually trustworthy. Most of all, thank You for Your beautiful "hesed" lavished on us every moment of every day, even when we can't see it and don't feel it. May we learn how to find our security solely in You as we trust Your plans for us and obey Your Word to us. Amen.

Focus Points

1. Keeping in mind our desire to enjoy a good relationship with a mother-in-law or daughter-in-law, if you have one, read Romans 12:9–21. For which command do you most need God's help to obey? (If you currently do not have a mother-in-law or daughter-in-law, answer this question by applying it to another important relationship in your life).
   List some action steps you will take this week to implement this directive.

2. According to Matthew 16:24–26 and Luke 14:33, what actions must we take to follow Jesus?

3. List some personal sacrifices required of us to obey these commands.
   Note: In Luke 14:33, Jesus is not asking us to give away all our possessions; rather, He is asking us to recognize who truly owns them and to assume the role of steward, instead of owner, realizing that all we have is on loan from our gracious God.

4. In the following verses, what does Jesus say is the reward for following Him?
   Matthew 16:25
   Mark 10:28–30
   John 8:12
   John 12:26

5. Spend some moments studying 1 Peter 2:20–25
   How did Jesus prove His absolute worthiness as the only One we should follow (verses 22–24)?

Before you committed to following Jesus, how are you described in verse 25?

6. As followers of Jesus, He is our Shepherd and the Guardian of our souls. If we're already following Him, why do we still need Him to be our Shepherd? Consider Psalm 23:1–4 as you frame your answer.

7. Based on Leviticus 25:18, what two things should we do to enjoy God's security?

8. When we make God's Word our guide and source of wisdom, what does Proverbs 3:23–24 promise?

9. Boaz prayed that Ruth would find refuge under God's wings. Read Psalm 91:1–4 and list the nouns used to describe God's security in these verses. For example: shelter, shadow, etc.

10. What are all the benefits found in Psalm 91:14–16 that are ours when we find security in God?
    Make this personal by rereading this passage out loud, inserting your name where applicable.

11. Ancient Israelites used to recite Psalm 121, entrusting themselves into God's care, as they ascended to Jerusalem to worship. As followers of Jesus, the truths about God in this passage apply to us as well. As you read through this short Psalm, which verse speaks most clearly to your heart, and why?

12. Psalm 36:5–10 showcases God's *hesed* in beautiful imagery. As you read these verses, picture the heavens, the skies, the mountains, and the oceans. In verses 7b–9, what should be our response to God's precious lovingkindness?

13. As you read Psalm 136:4–9 and 25, list some of the tangible proofs you see everyday indicating that God's lovingkindness is everlasting.
    Psalm 136 traces some of Israel's history. Why is it important to keep rehearsing God's everlasting lovingkindness as we connect it to events in our everyday lives?

14. In Ephesians 3:14–21, Paul offers a glimpse into his deep prayer life as he interceded for beloved believers in the church at Ephesus. Take a moment to pray this prayer out loud, inserting your name where appropriate. This is also a wonderful prayer guide to use in praying for family members.

15. How secure is God's *hesed* according to Isaiah 54:10?
    Let this truth become a lasting reminder that the worst catastrophe we could ever go through can never change or dilute God's unconditional lovingkindness that He delights to continually lavish upon us.

II

Hannah: Praying Power

So, how's your prayer life? This convicting question can instantly make us squirm. We all feel as though we don't pray often enough, fervently enough, or effectively enough. When our prayers aren't answered how we think they should be, or when we think they should be, we become discouraged and question the will of God regarding our requests. We are pulled in so many different directions as family demands, work responsibilities, unending daily tasks, and social media all demand our attention, leaving little time for prayer. We start to pray, but errant thoughts can sabotage our best intentions, diverting our focus. Worry over family members, finances, politics, employment, and health can easily overwhelm us, derailing our desire to commune with our God. Convicted, we compile long lists of prayer requests and then struggle with carving time out of our day to pray for them.

We know prayer is powerful, and that God can accomplish mighty and miraculous things when we pray, but we long to experience more of its power in our daily lives. We are drawn to those we know who, through the discipline of prayer, have become mighty prayer warriors. One such prayer warrior, a woman named Hannah, never ceases to amaze and encourage me each time I engage with her through the pages of Scripture. Praying changed her life. As we examine her story, we will discover five ways in which prayer can become powerfully life-changing for us as well.

We meet this remarkable woman and her family in 1 Samuel, chapters 1 and 2. Hannah and her husband Elkanah resided in the hill country of Ephraim, in a town called Ramah, about five miles north of Jerusalem. Even though Elkanah is referred to as an Ephraimite in verse 1, according to 1 Chronicles 6:33–38 he was also a Levite. As a direct descendant of Levi, Elkanah was legitimately qualified to function in a priestly capacity.[45] Elkanah had two wives: Hannah, *grace*,[46] and Peninnah, *coral* or *ruby*.[47] We discover at the beginning of her story that Hannah suffered from barrenness, while fertile Peninnah had given Elkanah children. We're not told how many but she is recorded as having sons and daughters, implying at least four children (1 Samuel 1:2, 4).

In Hannah's day, women validated their existence as females, and maintained their status in communities, based on their fertility. Both men and women considered it an absence of God's blessing when they experienced infertility. It must have been a devastating blow to discover her inability to conceive and then another crushing hardship to have to share her husband with a woman who happened to be fertile, capable of giving Elkanah something she could not—children.

Imagine Hannah's daily life. She had to share her husband in every way. Maybe you've seen some documentaries providing a glimpse into the homes of modern-day polygamous families. On one such program, I watched the husband seek the supportive approval of his first wife as the family prepared to incorporate a fourth wife. They called each other "sister-wives." The cameras recorded every emotion of the first wife during this tense process. Even though the first wife claimed to agree with their unusual lifestyle, she admitted it never got easier and that she suffered from jealousy, anger, and insecurity almost daily.

Hannah suffered intensely, living in close proximity to a woman who effortlessly gave birth, nursed, and raised children year after year. These two women were not friends and definitely not "sisters." Tensions ran high in that household as Peninnah habitually ridiculed, taunted, and harassed Hannah. "Her rival, however, would provoke her bitterly to irritate her, because the Lord had closed her womb. It happened year after year, as often as she went up to the house of the Lord, she would provoke her; so she wept and would not eat" (1 Samuel 1:6–7).

At least once a year, Elkanah travelled with his wives and children to Shiloh, a place where Joshua had set up the tabernacle of Moses, otherwise known as the tent of meeting (Joshua 18:1). I'll never forget the first time I toured an exact replica (dimension-wise) of the tabernacle located in Timnah in southern Israel. As I walked all around it and through it, I marveled at its significance in Israel's history. Our guide began in the outer court, explaining the significance of each part of the tabernacle to our tour group. As we worked our way toward the inner sanctum and parted the curtain veiling the holy of holies, I felt a hush come over everyone as we gazed at a replica of the ark of the covenant, remembering the holiness of this room in Israel's history. Only the high priest could enter this sacred room, and then only once a year on the Day of Atonement (Leviticus 16:2). In Hannah's era, the tabernacle stood out as the tallest structure around, and going there to worship symbolized a momentous event for Hannah and her family. Knowing that the ark of the covenant resided inside the holy of holies would have filled her with awe.

It was here in Shiloh, at the tabernacle, that Elkanah offered sacrifices when the family worshipped. Eli and his sons, Hophni and

Phineas, served as priests during Hannah's day. Eli descended from Ithamar, the youngest son of Aaron.[48] It's interesting to note that Eli, whose name means, *exalted is the Lord*,[49] gave his sons Egyptian names, Hophni *tadpole* and Phineas *the Nubian*.[50] Nubia comprised the region of southern Egypt and northern Sudan. Sadly, Eli's sons were considered "worthless men" who despised their sacred role and disregarded all of God's instructions for handling sacrificial meat and performing other priestly duties (1 Samuel 2:12–17).

When it came time for Elkanah to offer sacrifices, "he would give portions to Peninnah his wife and to all her sons and her daughters; but to Hannah he would give a double portion, for he loved Hannah, but the Lord had closed her womb" (1 Samuel 1:4–5). Elkanah's distribution of food undoubtedly galled Peninnah, who increased her torture of Hannah during the feasts at Shiloh. We notice something so important that it's repeated in verses five and six: God had closed Hannah's womb. The One who created us always remains in charge of His creation, even when we don't understand His timing or His ways. Hannah suffered terribly for something out of her control.

"Her rival, however, would provoke her bitterly to irritate her, because the Lord had closed her womb" (1 Samuel 1:6). Peninnah's anger over being the less-loved, less-favored wife manifested itself in vitriolic hatred toward Hannah. Peninnah knew exactly how to drive those deadly daggers deep into Hannah's soul. Perhaps Peninnah obtained perverse pleasure in watching Hannah's tearful reactions to her attacks. Year after year, every single time they "went up to the house of the Lord, she would provoke her; so she wept and would not eat" (1 Samuel 1:7). Maybe Peninnah even ridiculed Hannah's name, which means favor or grace, and reminded her that God had not shown her any. Perhaps Peninnah belittled Hannah for remaining infertile, making her feel less of a woman compared with her ability to produce multiple children. Maybe Hannah's close walk with God infuriated and convicted Peninnah. Certainly, Peninnah's abuse in all its forms marred those sacred and special pilgrimages to Shiloh to worship the Lord. Those who have ever suffered unjustly can resonate with Hannah's deep sorrow. She couldn't control how Elkanah demonstrated his love for her, and she couldn't control her own fertility. It's no wonder she lost her appetite and failed to hide her desperate tears.

Elkanah, bothered to see his beloved Hannah so upset, sad, and unable to even eat, said to her, "Hannah, why do you weep and why do you not eat and why is your heart sad? Am I not better to you than ten sons?" (1 Samuel 1:8). You can't fault Elkanah for trying to comfort Hannah and reminding her of how much he loved her. But that was not the problem. The problem was her infertility, coupled with Peninnah's painful reminders. Elkanah could do nothing about her barrenness because God had closed her womb. Perhaps he could have done something about Peninnah's relentless taunting, but maybe he chose not to get in the middle of the ongoing conflict.

We have instances throughout Scripture where we encounter women who desperately wanted to conceive but were unable to do so. Several famous women labeled as barren did not remain so forever because God miraculously opened their wombs. Sarah was called barren, but in her old age gave birth to Isaac (Genesis 11:30). Rebekah was called barren, but God answered Isaac's prayers and she gave birth to twin boys: Jacob and Esau (Genesis 25:21). Rachel was called barren, but God opened her womb as proof that He had not forgotten her plight, giving her Joseph and Benjamin (Genesis 29:31; 30:22). Elizabeth was called barren, but in her sunset years God enabled her to give birth to John the Baptist (Luke 1:7, 36).

I know women who have struggled with infertility. Some have borne children with medical help and others have adopted or become foster parents. I've noticed, however, that the broken-heartedness of barrenness has never alienated any of my believing friends from the Lord. In fact, the reverse has happened. As I've watched these precious women seek the Lord and pour over His Word, they've only grown stronger in their faith and closer to God, becoming strong prayer warriors.

Apparently, Elkanah's words encouraged Hannah to some extent, or perhaps she wanted to appease him, because in the next verse she is recorded as eating and drinking. "Then Hannah rose after eating and drinking in Shiloh" (1 Samuel 1:9a). Food and drink didn't solve her problem—they never do. She needed spiritual sustenance, not physical. So Hannah left her family and walked to the tabernacle. "Now Eli the priest was sitting on the seat by the doorpost of the temple of the Lord" (1 Samuel 1:9b). "Hannah is portrayed as the most pious woman in the Old Testament. Here she is shown going up to the Lord's house; no other woman in the Old Testament is mentioned as doing this."[51]

As Hannah approached the tabernacle, "she, greatly distressed, prayed to the Lord and wept bitterly" (1 Samuel 1:10). She didn't run to Eli, fall at his feet, and pour out her troubled soul. Nor did she seek to connect with the Lord through her Levitical husband. Instead, she ran to the Lord on her own, not ashamed to reveal her anguish in the form of bitter tears. There at the tabernacle in front of Eli, and perhaps others congregated there, Hannah made a vow to the Lord. In Hannah's day, a vow represented an offer to pay God for help He would give. They were serious commitments. Once made, they had to be fulfilled. According to Numbers 30:6–8, a husband could cancel his wife's vow on the day he found out about it. Hannah risked much to connect with her God.

Hannah's prayerful vow began by referencing God as the "Lord of hosts." The first time we see this title for God is in 1 Samuel 1:3, and the first time it's used in addressing God directly is in Hannah's prayer to Him (verse 11). By calling God this name, Hannah acknowledged that He is all-powerful, in charge of vast hosts of heavenly armies, and sovereign over everyone. He is in control of everything and able to perform anything He pleases. "The Lord of hosts, *Jehovah Sabaoth*, is the name of God we find used in Scripture when a man or woman is at the end of their rope so to speak. Jehovah Sabaoth is the strong tower which God has made available for those times when we fail and are powerless, when our resources are inadequate, when there is no other help."[52]

Hannah and her people believed that the Lord of hosts sat above the cherubim on the ark of the covenant (1 Samuel 4:4). That's one of the reasons why the Israelites wanted the ark to accompany them into battle to give them victory, and why it was so devastating when enemies captured it. As Hannah prayed that day in the tabernacle, perhaps she envisioned the ark of the covenant that resided within the holy of holies, just yards away from her. Hannah prayerfully vowed, "O Lord of hosts, if you will look with compassion on the suffering of your female servant, remembering me and not forgetting your servant, and give a male child to your servant, then I will dedicate him to the Lord all the days of his life. His hair will never be cut" (1 Samuel 1:11, NET).

Interestingly, "Hannah is the only woman shown making and fulfilling a vow to the Lord; she is also the only woman who is specifically said to pray."[53] Hannah asked God to look with compassion on her suffering, to consider all she had endured because of her barrenness. She wanted God to feel her pain. In the asking lay the awareness that God saw her, knew her plight, and could act with compassion on her behalf. Hannah felt so forgotten and alone. She asked God to show that He remembered her by opening her womb. She called herself a servant three times in this prayer, acknowledging her relationship with Almighty God as the only one powerful enough to control her life. Even though Hannah had not yet experienced God's compassion regarding her closed womb, that didn't make Him any less compassionate, nor any less powerful. She knew to the depths of her being that her Lord of hosts saw her barrenness, and she trusted He would look with compassion on her situation.

She specifically asked for a little boy because she wanted to dedicate her child to serve Him. If God chose to bless her with a baby boy, she, in turn, wanted to bless God by giving her son up for His service. She promised that her son would be set apart to serve the Lord all the days of his life. If Hannah wanted a child for the sole purpose of removing the stigma of barrenness, she would not have so unselfishly vowed to give him up. Her motives, as revealed in her prayer, show a higher regard for God's purposes than for her own. As an astute woman, she recognized the disintegrating spiritual climate and the worthlessness of Eli's sons as priests. She wanted to be part of the solution and she trusted her future son could be a catalyst for change.

In addition, Hannah promised her little boy would observe the vow of the Nazirite. The Nazirite vow was threefold: first, those undertaking the vow could not drink wine or any other fermented drink. They could not even drink grape juice or eat raisins. Second, they could not cut their hair. Third, they could not go near a dead body because that would make them ceremonially unclean. Even if an immediate family member died, they couldn't go near the body.

The vow's visible signs typified inner consecration. Men or women could voluntarily take the vow and it was usually for a set period of time (Numbers 6). If Hannah intended her baby to observe the vow in utero, then she would also be keeping the vow's dietary restrictions during her pregnancy.

As a deeply anguished Hannah prayed to the Lord, lips moving soundlessly, she successfully captured Eli's attention, all right! "Now Hannah was speaking from her heart. Although her lips were moving, her voice was inaudible" (1 Samuel 1:12–13, NET). Eli had no idea what she was saying, so based on her unusual behavior the priest decided she must be inebriated. He rebuked her for getting drunk and told her to put away her wine (1 Samuel 1:13–14). How sad that he didn't recognize a praying woman. Maybe drunkenness during the feasts was more common than fervent prayer! One author noted, "Here, as elsewhere, Eli is portrayed as a man unable to distinguish appearance from reality, as a man who lacked substance. Though Eli was the high priest of Shiloh—and ostensibly a man of exceptional spiritual maturity, he is consistently depicted as spiritually blind and inert. He was a man who watched lips instead of perceiving hearts, who judged profound spirituality to be profligate indulgence in wine, who heard nothing when the Lord spoke and who criticized his sons for abusing the sacrificial system yet grew fat from their take."[54]

Hannah needed to set Eli straight. She responded to his accusation by saying, "That's not the way it is, my lord! I am under a great deal of stress. I have drunk neither wine nor beer. Rather, I have poured out my soul to the Lord. Don't consider your servant a wicked woman, for until now I have spoken from my deep pain and anguish" (1 Samuel 1:15–16, NET). Even in her disclaimer to Eli, Hannah demonstrated respect worthy of his priestly office, despite his misguided assumptions. Hannah clarified her sobriety. Instead of resorting to temporary diversions or numbing fillers, such as alcohol, to deal with the tremendous stress in her life, she turned to her God and poured out her soul to Him. Hannah wanted Eli to revise his false opinion of her, but she also wanted him to know that deep pain and anguish fueled her prayers. Our most authentic prayers often rise from utter desperation. When we're in great distress, we don't rely on formal phrases or trite recitations to communicate with God. We get to the heart of the matter just as Hannah did, as layers of pretense are stripped away. "Eli replied, 'Go in peace, and may the God of Israel grant the request that you have asked of him.' She said, 'May I, your servant, find favor in your sight.' So the woman went her way and got something to eat. Her face no longer looked sad" (1 Samuel 1:17–18, NET).

Because Hannah believed with all her heart that God had heard and that He would answer, her burden lifted and her face reflected the change. In the same way, we have the wonderful privilege of pouring out our heartaches and disappointments to the Lord. We can rise from our knees with lighter hearts and confident spirits, certain that God has heard and will act on our behalf. When our boys were little, they quickly tired of carrying a burden any kind of distance. Often, before I fully realized it, I had absent-mindedly allowed them to transfer backpacks, books, jackets, and even toys into my arms. That's exactly what I do. I come to God burdened, and He graciously takes my burden from me in this great exchange called prayer. Hannah could rejoin her family with her huge burden lifted, the tears wiped from her face, fully confident her Lord of hosts would answer.

Once home, Elkanah slept with Hannah and the Lord "remembered her." The Hebrew phrase used here for remembered has the sense of considering needs or desires with favor and kindness.[55] How wonderful that God showed favor to one whose name meant favor! What a joyous day when Hannah gave birth to a healthy baby boy and held this tangible proof of answered prayer in her arms! Hannah "named him Samuel, thinking, 'I asked the Lord for him'" (1 Samuel 1:20, NET). The name Samuel has the connotation of *heard of God* or *asked of God*.[56] With the stigma of infertility removed, Hannah could hold and nurse and love her own baby.

Because Hannah's prayer in front of Eli was inaudible, we may wonder how it came to be recorded in Scripture? Since all of God's Word is inspired, this is proof that God heard her every word. Perhaps Hannah recounted this prayer to Samuel and others as part of the testimony of God's grace in her life. In addition, perhaps she explained to Samuel exactly why he had to live under the Nazirite vow when she told him about her promise to God and the importance of keeping it. We can imagine him as a little boy eyeing some sweet, juicy grapes on someone else's plate, wanting to taste them, but knowing he could not.

When the next feast date rolled around, Elkanah prepared to take his entire family once again to Shiloh to offer sacrifices. He probably assumed Hannah and baby Samuel would accompany them. When Hannah explained that she would stay at home with the boy until he was weaned, Elkanah saw the wisdom in her decision. He said, "Do what you think best" (1 Samuel 1:23, NET). The fact that he allowed her to make such a bold commitment shows how much he respected her walk with God. However, he cautioned, "Only let the Lord establish His word" (1 Samuel 1:23, NKJV). Another translation reads, "May the Lord help you keep your promise" (NLT). Her husband knew how difficult and heart-wrenching Hannah's decision would be for her. He recognized she would need divine help to keep her vow to the Lord. Because Hannah had promised to give Samuel to the Lord's service in Shiloh, she would be fulfilling her vow by leaving her boy behind, returning home without him.

In Hannah's day, women nursed their little ones for approximately three years.[57] We can imagine just how precious those few years were to Hannah, knowing she soon would be giving him up. Perhaps she, like Mary, the mother of Jesus, treasured every moment of those fleeting years in her heart. When the momentous day arrived to deliver Samuel to his new home in Shiloh, Hannah resolutely followed through with her vow. Women who have given up babies for adoption, or whose tragic life circumstances have forced their child into the foster system, can best identify with Hannah's feelings in separating from little Samuel. Hannah and her family traveled to Shiloh bringing "a three-year-old bull and one ephah of flour and a jug of wine" (1 Samuel 1:24). Hannah could not peer into her future. She had no idea God would give her more children. In her mind, she was giving her only child to the Lord.

As she presented her precious little boy to Eli, she reminded the priest that she was the woman who had stood next to him more than three years ago. She said to Eli, "Oh, my lord! As your soul lives, my lord, I am the woman who stood here beside you, praying to the Lord. For this boy I prayed, and the Lord has given me my petition which I asked of Him. So I have also dedicated him to the Lord; as long as he lives he is dedicated to the Lord" (1 Samuel 1:26–28).

One friend insightfully commented on Hannah's prayer when she wrote, "The words 'asked' and 'dedicated' are the same word in Hebrew. I wonder if the word play shows Hannah's view of prayer as being twofold: it's something we ask of God and it's our response when He answers. Hannah's prayer seemed to focus not just on what she wanted God to do to make her situation better, but also on what her personal response would be to His answer. It's interesting to note that she was willing to give God nothing less than what He had given her. She entrusted Him with what was most precious because she realized her most precious gift was from Him. For her, nothing was off limits to God."[58]

Hannah, a devoted mother, must have surveyed Samuel's new home with sharp eyes and keen observation. Perhaps she made sure his little bed had enough blankets and was close enough to Eli to ensure protection. Maybe she instructed Eli on how best to care for her little boy, describing what he liked to eat, what he couldn't eat based on the Nazirite vow, and tips on how best to discipline him according to his personality. Amazingly, she would be entrusting her son's care into the hands of one who had failed as a father in bringing up his own boys.

Not only were Eli's two sons, Hophni and Phinehas, worthless and disobedient, they were also wickedly perverted. They were not ashamed to engage in sex with the women who served at the doorway of the tabernacle (1 Samuel 2:22). This practice had overtones of pagan Canaanite cultic practices with shrine or temple prostitutes. "Perhaps these women were Nazirites involved in volunteer service at the worship site, or they may have been cultic prostitutes. However, they were being treated as though they were pagan shrine prostitutes."[59] Eli tried to get his wayward sons to stop all their evil activities, but they refused to listen.

What was supposed to be taking place at the door or entrance to the tabernacle? The priests were commanded to offer a lamb as a burnt offering; one in the morning and one in the evening, every day continually (Exodus 29:38–42). Why? Because then God would meet them there, and His glorious presence would sanctify the tabernacle. If they obeyed His commands, God promised to dwell among the children of Israel and be their powerful, prayer-answering God.

No wonder Hannah viewed the tabernacle as a place that should be holy, a place where she could appeal to God who answers prayers.

In these modern times, before children can be placed into foster care or adopted, several intense home studies are conducted on the prospective parents, as well as the home environment. If conditions are less than optimal, the child's placement can be jeopardized. Imagine doing a home study on Eli's family! As a mother and a grandmother, it astounds me that Hannah placed her tender and impressionable three-year-old son into this dysfunctional and corrupt environment. That she could leave him there, only to see him once a year, showcases a woman whose faith and trust in God reached heroic proportions. Mark and I are blessed to have six grandchildren; one who is currently three years old. My heart breaks when I put myself in Hannah's shoes and think about sending our little grandson into this kind of environment. Hannah's faith in God's sovereign protection for her sweet son amazes me.

Samuel ministered before the Lord wearing a miniature version of a priest's linen ephod, a sleeveless, apron-like garment worn over a robe.[60] Because Elkanah belonged to the tribe of Levi, Samuel, also a Levite, could minister as a priest before the Lord. That is why he could legitimately wear a linen ephod and sleep in the tabernacle. "Samuel's mother annually brought Samuel a robe *(mĕ'îl)*, a longer outer garment worn by members of the Levitical tribe involved in priestly service. This thoughtful gift from Hannah suggests that although Samuel was gone from the household in Ramah, he was still very much in Hannah's heart. Through the use of the clothing motif in portraying Samuel's career, the writer suggests that Samuel's life was the outcome of a splendid mother of faith."[61] Each time Hannah brought a new robe to Samuel, she may have marveled at how much he had grown. She would have needed to estimate how big to make the next year's garment for her precious firstborn son. Along with her son's physical growth, Hannah would have marveled at his spiritual growth as verified in 1 Samuel 2:26, "Now the boy Samuel was growing up and finding favor both with the Lord and with people."

As Hannah interacted with her son, at least once a year if not more, she would have rejoiced in the relationship Samuel enjoyed with her Lord of hosts. "Samuel grew up 'in the presence of the Lord,' literally, 'with Yahweh.' This Hebrew phrase is used in the Torah to describe Moses' position when he received the Decalogue (Exodus 34:28). In Psalm (130:7) 'with Yahweh' is said to be a place of 'unfailing love' and 'full redemption.' In the present context it seems to suggest that Samuel enjoyed a childhood marked by divine favor and a lifestyle evidencing a Moses-like relationship with the Lord."[62] How that must have comforted Hannah's mother-heart! Her son was in the best of hands—God's hands.

After giving up her son, the Lord graciously attended to Hannah, enabling her to conceive and birth three more sons and two daughters (1 Samuel 2:21). God continued to shower His grace and favor on this precious woman who loved Him so much and gave up her firstborn son for Him. I also love it that the sharp arrows in Peninnah's arsenal were rendered ineffective as the object of her abuse now had sons and daughters of her own!

We are privileged to learn from this woman of faith whose prayer contained eighteen recorded utterances of the Lord's name. Hannah knew and loved her God! From her beautiful petition in 1 Samuel 2:1–10, delivered right after she fulfilled her vow to the Lord, we can discover five ways in which prayer benefitted Hannah, and how prayer benefits us in powerful and concrete ways. Each application will suggest a tangible way to apply it to our lives in what I will call a "power of prayer action step."

God's deliverance gives me victory.

> *My heart rejoices in the Lord! The Lord has made me strong. Now I have an answer for my enemies; I rejoice because you rescued me* (1 Samuel 2:1, NLT).

Hannah praised God for deliverance from past hurts and victory over those who had hurt her. Despite leaving her little boy in Shiloh and returning home without him, Hannah could still be joyful because her joy remained sourced in the Lord, not in her circumstances. Her Lord of hosts made her strong. Only He could enable Hannah to keep her vow by delivering Samuel into Eli's care. She rejoiced because God had given her victory over the heartache of infertility. Her enemy, Peninnah, had been silenced, and due to God's deliverance, Hannah could be joyful instead of tearful in her presence.

Some years ago, I suffered an unjust attack from another believer. This person shared their anger with a friend and the situation escalated. Now I have done many wrong things, but in this case, I didn't think I had sinned. In tears, I asked my Lord of hosts to protect me from their sharp words piercing my soul. When one of the women called to chastise me, and request a meeting, the first words out of my mouth were, "This doesn't sound like a happy meeting!" I pictured myself hiding under God's wings and letting Him fight this battle for me. I strongly sensed the Lord leading me to humbly ask their forgiveness for any way I had offended them and refrain from defending myself. This diffused their anger and they canceled our meeting. I still remember the sense of awe I felt that God had indeed rescued me.

Perhaps there is something in your life right now that has you feeling defeated. Maybe it's a difficult relationship, or a wayward child, or a conflict at work, or ongoing health issues, or financial worries. ***A power of prayer action step*** to take is first rehearse past victories when you experienced God's deliverance. Next, focus on praising Him for all the ways He has protected, delivered, and provided victory for you in the past. Then, commit this present difficult situation to your Lord of hosts, asking Him to fight this battle for you, praying He will show Himself strong on your behalf, making you stronger in the process, and allowing the victory to glorify Him.

God's strength gives me shelter.

> *No one is holy like the Lord! There is no one besides you; there is no Rock like our God* (1 Samuel 2:2, NLT).

Hannah recognized there is only one true God and He remained her only source of strength and place of refuge. Hannah praised God's uniqueness, strength, and divine protection. Publically recognizing God's attributes and actions strengthened her faith. In her despair over her infertility, and under the barrage of Peninnah's relentless attacks, she ran to the tabernacle, ran to God, and there found the strength to go on.

Mark and I used to own a sweet mixed-breed dog named Daffodil. We called her Daffy for short. Since we rescued her from the animal shelter as an adult dog, we had no control over how she was raised. We soon learned that she feared several things, one of them being thunderstorms. Even though she had a perfectly comfortable place to sleep near our bed, that wasn't good enough when a storm hit. She would find my side of the bed, carefully climb in with me, and press her trembling body as closely as she could to mine while I reassured her. I'm just like Daffodil. When the storms of life hit, the only way I can stay calm and stop trembling is by pressing close to my God and hearing reassurance from His Word. His perfect strength is my only safe shelter.

One of my dearest friends adopted a five-year-old child. Sadly, this boy never fully bonded with my friend and her husband. As he grew, he acted out in all sorts of harmful ways that broke their hearts. He left home, an angry young man. He soon got into so much trouble he was incarcerated. Shortly after this, my friend asked to meet with me on a regular basis for encouragement. We sorrowed together and prayed together. She began writing out Scripture verses on index cards, keeping them in her purse, and pulling them out whenever the storm threatened to overcome her. Clinging to God and keeping His Word uppermost in her mind helped her cope with this difficult situation.

Perhaps you're in a storm right now and longing for someplace safe to land. When we're in any kind of storm, everything around us seems shaky and unsettled and we can feel overwhelmed by the smallest things. *A power of prayer action step* we could take is to spend some concentrated time in God's Word. Using a concordance or a Bible reference website, look up verses that talk about God being our refuge and strength. Choose some of these verses to write on index cards to keep in a purse, or tape to a bathroom mirror, or enter them into a phone or computer. When the waves threaten to pull us under, we have verses in our arsenal ready to read and put into practice. We can ask God to strengthen our hearts as we choose to shelter ourselves inside the truth of His promises to us.

God's sovereign control gives me confidence.

> *Stop acting so proud and haughty! Don't speak with such arrogance! For the Lord is a God who knows what you have done; He will judge your actions* (1 Samuel 2:3, NLT).

Hannah did not mention Peninnah's name, but we may wonder if she had Peninnah in mind based on what she prayed. Hannah knew she could leave retribution for Peninnah's horrible actions in God's righteous hands. God knew every word Peninnah had said and everything she had done to hurt Hannah. Hannah resolved to let God be the Judge.

> *The bow of the mighty is now broken, and those who stumbled are now strong* (1 Samuel 2:4, NLT).

With infertility behind her, Hannah knew that Peninnah's bow was broken and her arrows of torment rendered useless. Hannah must have viewed Peninnah's proclivity to bear children as an area of great strength, and her barren state as one of weakness and defect. How the tables had turned!

> *Those who were well fed are now starving, and those who were starving are now full. The childless woman now has seven children, and the woman with many children wastes away* (1 Samuel 2:5, NLT).

Hannah conceded Peninnah's wealth in the form of children brought fulfillment to her as a woman. She, on the other hand, felt starved for children to validate her full worth as a woman in the eyes of her

culture. But with the birth of Samuel, Hannah could gratefully identify with the formerly childless woman who now had seven children.
The number seven is used here in an ideal sense. Elsewhere in the
Old Testament, having seven children equates fertility with God's
blessing on a family (Jeremiah 15:9 and Ruth 4:15).[63] Hannah, especially sensitized to the downtrodden, the despairing, and the helpless,
resonated with others experiencing barrenness. She could empathize
with all their fluctuating emotions. Hannah's confidence increased
exponentially when God intervened to enable her to conceive, and
she who had been low in the eyes of Peninnah and society, was now
lifted up. Perhaps Hannah watched Peninnah "wasting away" as
the bitter anger and hatred she once spewed in Hannah's direction
turned inward and began wreaking havoc on her own health.

Hannah's high view of God led her to praise the way He ruled
His creation: She praised the Lord because He knows and evaluates
everything. He controls wins, losses, food, hunger, money, fertility,
birth, life and death, status, and all creation. It's almost like Hannah
took a huge step back and observed life from every angle and level as
she watched what a knowing and evaluating God does with mankind
and creation. We can see the paradoxes and exchanges here—the
throwing down, and the lifting up:

*The Lord gives both death and life; He brings some down to the grave
but raises others up. The Lord makes some poor and others rich; He
brings some down and lifts others up. He lifts the poor from the dust
and the needy from the garbage dump. He sets them among princes,
placing them in seats of honor. For all the earth is the Lord's, and he
has set the world in order* (1 Samuel 2:6–8, NLT).

One of my relatives suffered the loss of a large sum of money when he unwittingly became the victim of a Ponzi scheme by trusting his misguided financial advisor. I found myself feeling angry with greedy, evil men who make their fortunes so fraudulently. It saddened me to know how this relative was hurt and robbed. However, I marveled at his confidence in the Lord in the face of such crippling financial loss. In one of our conversations he reminded me that at the end of the day, God is still in control. He told another family member, "I used to have my bank account and Jesus, now I just have Jesus and that's enough for me!"

Maybe you're going through a situation right now that is rocking your world. Perhaps you're even tempted to doubt God could ever fix it. We can feel powerless and hopeless in difficult circumstances and we may despair that God could ever intervene on our behalf in a timely way. *A power of prayer action step* to practice is to remember that we can only control our own actions and reactions. Much as we'd like to, we can't control anyone else's actions or reactions. We may need to sit down in a quiet place and place our hands in a fisted position palm-side-up on our knees. As we acknowledge God as the Sovereign Controller of everything, we can open our hands to symbolize relinquishing control that doesn't belong to us, but to God. One writer advised, "Hold everything in your hands lightly, otherwise it hurts when God pries your fingers open."[64] As we release what we've been grasping so tightly to God, acknowledging His right to rule, and asking for the faith to trust how He will deal with our situation, then we will experience His divine help to wait patiently according to His timetable, instead of our own.

God's prevailing protection gives me peace.

> *He will protect his faithful ones, but the wicked will disappear in darkness. No one will succeed by strength alone* (1 Samuel 2:9, NLT).

Hannah praised God for differentiating between believers and unbelievers. Without a doubt, Hannah's greatest desire was that Samuel be one of God's faithful ones, experiencing His divine protection. As Samuel increased in favor with God and all the people, Hannah rejoiced at the vivid contrast between her godly son and Eli's wicked sons, thankful their evil behavior had not corrupted her child.

What a comfort to know that God watches over every step we take and every decision we make. As believers in Jesus, we have the promised protection of His presence in every part of our lives. Even in the most frightening situations, God's protection is all encompassing. Mark and I lived in Portland, Oregon while he earned two master's degrees from Western Seminary. One winter weekend, Mark was invited to preach in a small church in Redmond, a town located on the eastern side of Oregon's Cascade Range. As we left Sunday night after church to drive back to Portland, we noticed snow falling steadily, but thought we could make it back with no problem. We had studded snow tires on our car, which we thought would give us enough traction. As we began our ascent over Mount Hood, the snowfall increased and visibility worsened. Suddenly, we could no longer see the edge of the curving mountain road, only the tips of fence posts flanking the edges. The narrow, winding road made it impossible at this point to turn around and we both began to pray out loud, begging God to help us.

Almost immediately, we sensed the Lord's presence in the car with us and felt unexplainable peace. We then noticed the red lights of a semitruck in front of us. In near blizzard-like conditions, we followed this truck all the way up the mountain, at times even losing sight of the lights for brief moments in the fierce snowstorm. The lights disappeared as we neared the summit of Mount Hood and the snow turned to rain. We came to a stop at a police roadblock that had been set up to halt traffic due to the dangerous weather. I will never forget the officer's comments to us that night. He asked us what we were doing on that road. We explained where we'd been and that we'd been following a semitruck's lights all the way up the mountain. With an amazed look on his face, probably thinking, *"These people are crazy!"* he said, "Folks, this road has been closed for hours. I promise you there have been no trucks on this road!" That's when we realized that God had sent those red lights for us to follow.

Perhaps you lack peace and are feeling vulnerable and unprotected. We can feel quite alone and unsupported at times. ***A power of prayer action step*** to take is to open our Bible to the Psalms—the middle—and place our photo inside the pages as a visual reminder that we stand on the bedrock of God's truth, which lasts forever. Then we can close our Bibles, keeping our picture inside as a reminder that our life is hidden in Christ. Nothing, absolutely nothing, can enter our life without the express permission of God, and when it does, it goes through Jesus first because, as believers, we are in Christ. Then we can spend some time in prayer thanking God for His prevailing protection and asking Him to flood our souls with His peace.

God's perfect plan for the future gives me hope.

> *Those who fight against the Lord will be shattered. He thunders against them from heaven; The Lord judges throughout the earth. He gives power to his king; He increases the strength of his anointed one* (1 Samuel 2:10, NLT).

Hannah praised God's perfect plans for our future. Enlightened by the Spirit of God, Hannah prophesied that Israel would someday have a king and eventually a Messiah. God's perfect plans would come to fruition in His perfect time. That gave Hannah hope then and it gives us hope now. Don't you love it that God will someday right all wrongs? One day every knee will bow and all of God's critics will be silenced forever (Philippians 2:10).

Mark underwent double knee replacement surgery some years ago. Most people have one knee replaced at a time. We didn't know what recovery and rehab would look like with both legs out of commission. A few days after surgery we met with an entire team of rehab therapists and heard their detailed plan for Mark's full recovery and mobility. Just knowing there was a plan in place and experts involved gave us great hope. The grueling rehab lasted for six weeks, but today Mark has excellent flexion in both knees and walks pain-free.

In our media-saturated culture, we notice the decline in values, eroding morals, rampant intolerance, and pagan overtones prevalent in our society. We can easily succumb to fear when we consider the ramifications of all that is happening around us. Revelation 21:1 reminds us that this world has been scheduled for replacement surgery. Just knowing that God has a perfect plan in place and that He will execute it when His time is right gives us great hope for the future. ***A power of prayer action step*** we could take is to make a list of everything we're worried about, either things in the present or something in the future, or even any regrets that still haunt us from our past. We might want to give voice to each worry or regret by saying them out loud. Then beside each item, we can place a check mark indicating that God has heard our concerns. In addition, beside each check mark we can write a little prescription sign—Rx, to remind us that God has a perfect plan already in place. As believers in Jesus, we can be assured that nothing is wasted in God's economy, even past events that bring regret, because God supernaturally causes all things in our lives to work together for our good and His glory (Romans 8:28). When we lay our burdens down at His feet, releasing them into His tender care, we know we can depend upon Him to fill our hearts with His peace, joy, and hope as we face a future free from debilitating fear.

Many years ago, another "Hannah" experienced the power of prayer in her own life as recorded in this true story: "How much does a prayer weigh? The only man I ever knew who tried to weigh one still does not know. Once upon a time he thought he did. That was when he owned a little grocery store on the West side. It was the week before Christmas after the World War. A tired-looking woman came into the store and asked him for enough food to make up a Christmas dinner for her children. He asked her how much she could afford to spend. She answered, 'My husband was killed in the war. I have nothing to offer but a little prayer.' This man confesses that he was not very sentimental in those days. A grocery store could not be run like a breadline. So he said, 'Write it on paper,' and turned about his business. To his surprise, the woman plucked a piece of paper out of her pocket and handed it to him over the counter and said, 'I did that during the night watching over my sick baby.'

The grocer took the paper before he could recover from his surprise, and then regretted having done so! For what would he do with it, what could he say? Then an idea suddenly came to him. He placed the paper, without even reading the prayer, on the weight side of his old-fashioned scales. He said, 'We shall see how much food this is worth.' To his astonishment the scale would not go down when he put a loaf of bread on the other side. To his confusion and embarrassment, it would not go down though he kept on adding food, anything he could lay his hands on quickly, because people were watching him. He tried to be gruff and he was making a bad job of it. His face got red and it made him angry to be flustered. So finally he said, 'Well, that's all the scales will hold anyway. Here's a bag. You'll have to put it in yourself. I'm busy.' With what sounded like a gasp or a little sob, she took the bag and started packing in the food, wiping her eyes on her sleeves every time her arm was free to do so. He tried not to look, but he could not help seeing that he had given her a pretty big bag and that it was not quite full. So he tossed a large cheese down the counter, but he did not say anything; nor did he see the timid smile of grateful understanding, which glistened in her moist eyes.

When the woman had gone, he went to look at the scales, scratching his head and shaking it in puzzlement. Then he found the solution. The scales were broken. The grocer is an old man now. His hair is white. But he still scratches it in the same place and shakes it slowly back and forth with the same puzzled expression. He knew it had not been just his imagination, for he still had the slip of paper upon which the woman's prayer had been written: 'Please, Lord, give us this day our daily bread' (Matthew 6:11)."[65]

Father God, thank You for the privilege of meeting Hannah through the pages of Your timeless Word. It's so encouraging to meet a woman whose deep faith and powerful prayer life continues to impact us today. As we deepen our faith-walk and expand our prayer life, may the eternal benefits we reap serve to edify us and encourage others. May we be ever thankful that Your divine deliverance gives us victory. In Your strength alone we find safe shelter. We can be confident because You are in sovereign control. Your pervasive presence and prevailing protection give us peace. We can live hope-filled lives because You have a perfect plan for our future. We love You. Amen.

Focus Points

1. From Romans 8:35–39, what are the seven difficulties listed in this passage?

2. Have you experienced any of these in your own life? If so, which one, or ones?

3. According to verse 37, how do we obtain victory, even when we're experiencing calamity?

4. Find ten things in verses 38–39 that cannot separate us from God's love. Elkanah asked Hannah if his love for her wasn't worth ten sons. Compared to capricious and quantifiable human love, God's ability to love is boundless. How can this reassure you today as you view a present difficulty in your life through this lens?

5. Psalm 91 beautifully details all the benefits we reap when we dwell in the shelter of the Most High. After reading this passage, which description resonates most with you and why?

6. Read Psalm 103:19. Thinking about something that is bothering you right now, how does this verse reassure you?

7. In Daniel 2:20–22, what does God possess?
   What does He change?
   What does He do with those in power?
   What does He reveal?

8. How does the scope and breadth of His sovereign control, as revealed in these verses, help change your perspective regarding something troubling you right now, over which you have no control?

8. Look up Psalm 91:9–11, Proverbs 2:7–8, and John 17:11 and 15. As you consider your journey so far, can you recall a time where you sensed God's protection in a supernatural way? Write it down as a prayer of praise to Him, ready to share with others.

9. Read Jeremiah 29:11; Psalm 33:10–11, and Proverbs 19:21 to answer the following questions:
    Are you a planner?
    Have your plans ever gone awry?
    Is God a planner?
    According to these verses, do His plans ever fail?
    What does God sometimes do with our human plans?

10. Since God is perfect, His plans are always perfect. How does knowing this truth influence your attitude about the future?

11. From Psalms 113 and 138, see how many verses you can find that describe Hannah's situation.
    In what ways can these same verses apply to your life?

12. Take some time to reread the ***power of prayer action steps*** under each application point and choose one or more to practice this week.

III

Abigail: Pleasing God

In our daily interactions with others, we may encounter people who seem almost too good to be true. We may notice their words and actions appear unselfish as they serve with humble grace. We observe their good attitudes under pressure and in adverse circumstances and wonder how they do it? Are they simply "people pleasers" putting up a good front? Do they plaster on a smile, go through the motions, but inwardly it's a different story? There's a girl in Scripture who seems almost too good to be true. What was her secret? Trapped in a miserable marriage and facing a bleak future, how in the world did she develop into a woman who pleased God with her attitude, words, and actions?

We meet this exemplary woman in 1 Samuel 25. "Now there was a man in Maon whose business was in Carmel; and the man was very rich, and he had three thousand sheep and a thousand goats. And it came about while he was shearing his sheep in Carmel (now the man's name was Nabal, and his wife's name was Abigail. And the woman was intelligent and beautiful in appearance, but the man was harsh and evil in his dealings, and he was a Calebite)" (1 Samuel 25:2–3). Abigail and Nabal resided in the town of Maon, a city in the western foothills of Judah. Nabal's business happened to be near Maon in the city of Carmel about seven miles south of Hebron. We assume Abigail originally hailed from Carmel because in 1 Samuel 27:3, she is called a "Carmelitess." It was in this region that Abigail first met David, a famous fugitive on the run from King Saul. In playing some serious hide-and-seek with Saul, David and his men had moved to the wilderness of Paran near Abigail's hometown of Carmel.

We might not expect a wealthy, prosperous man to be named Nabal, which means *foolish* or *senseless*.[66] And yet, based on this man's actions as observed in the text, his name aptly described him. Abigail's husband is depicted as "harsh and evil in his dealings" (1 Samuel 25:3). He may have been rich, but wealth is no guarantee of wisdom or righteous behavior! In stark contrast to her husband, Abigail is described as "intelligent and beautiful in appearance" (1 Samuel 25:3). The reference to Nabal being a Calebite clues us in to the fact that he was one of David's kinsmen. "The Calebite clan, an esteemed family in Judah, was apparently responsible for the founding of David's hometown of Bethlehem."[67]

We may wonder about Abigail's daily existence, married to this harsh and evil man. Based on his character, it's not a stretch to think he may have been an abusive husband, if not physically, at least verbally and emotionally. How could Abigail even communicate with such a hard, evil, vile-tempered man? A man like that is incapable of expressing love or kindness. You may as well forget about any displays of tenderness or romance from this guy! Harsh words and brutal demeanor can hurt feelings and crush spirits, as Abigail may have frequently experienced!

We question her dad's motives in choosing this kind of man for his amazing daughter. Maybe he coveted someone rich for a son-in-law and believed his daughter would be amply provided for. Perhaps he gained financially from arranging Abigail's marriage to Nabal. We may wonder if he ever regretted orchestrating his beautiful daughter's marriage to Nabal. We're not told how many years Abigail suffered, married to this cruel and evil man, but the luxurious life his great wealth provided could hardly have compensated for his lack of love and warmth.

One day, David heard that Nabal was shearing his sheep. Sheep shearing times were celebrated with feasting and gift giving.[68] They may have occurred twice a year, in the spring and early fall.[69] David and his six hundred men had been hanging out with Nabal's men in the desert, befriending them and protecting them from frequent Philistine raids. As fugitives hiding from King Saul, David and his company would have been in constant need of food and supplies. So when David heard about Nabal shearing his sheep, he sent ten of his young men with the following message: "Have a long life, peace be to you, and peace be to your house, and peace be to all that you have. Now I have heard that you have shearers; now your shepherds have been with us and we have not insulted them, nor have they missed anything all the days they were in Carmel. Ask your young men and they will tell you. Therefore let my young men find favor in your eyes, for we have come on a festive day. Please give whatever you find at hand to your servants and to your son David" (1 Samuel 25:6–8).

David stressed the word "peace" three times in his message to Nabal. He indicated he had timed his request to coincide with the shearing event. David knew this occasion would include generosity in the form of food and drink as households celebrated success with their flocks (2 Samuel 13:23–24). Since he and his men had treated Nabal's servants with respect and had protected Nabal's enterprise, it seemed only logical to expect a measure of reciprocity for services rendered. He asked for kindness from Nabal by generously sharing some provisions with him and his men. David simply asked for whatever surplus Nabal had on hand. He didn't want his request to be burdensome. He finished his plea by calling himself Nabal's son; an ingratiating term designed to engender a sympathetic response.

But Nabal, true to his cruel and foolish nature responded, "Who is David? And who is the son of Jesse? There are many servants today who are each breaking away from his master. Shall I then take my bread and my water and my meat that I have slaughtered for my shearers, and give it to men whose origin I do not know?" (1 Samuel 25:10–11). It's hard to believe Nabal did not know anything about David given his notoriety throughout the land as one who had killed a Philistine giant named Goliath (1 Samuel 17). However, he may have considered himself as more important than anyone else due to his great wealth and prominence in the region. In Nabal's eyes, David was simply a runaway servant; not worthy of his consideration. Nabal's use of the personal pronoun "my" four times in his response to David revealed his self-centeredness and unwillingness to share what belonged to him with others. Nabal's careless and cruel words would have aroused righteous indignation, igniting passions for revenge and punishment. As they used to say in the old Wild West, "Them's fightin' words!"

David's young men turned and left Nabal's presence to return to their wilderness camp, no doubt incensed by such a blatant rejection of their beloved leader. Their anger probably escalated as they rehashed the terrible insults embedded in Nabal's response. With the message delivered, in all its ugliness, David shouted to his men, "Each of you gird on his sword!" as he strapped on his own. Then four hundred men started off on the warpath with David while two hundred remained behind to guard their equipment (1 Samuel 25:12–13).

Meanwhile, one of Nabal's servants ran to Abigail to warn her, "David sent messengers from the wilderness to greet our master, and he scorned them. Yet the men were very good to us, and we were not insulted, nor did we miss anything as long as we went about with them, while we were in the fields. They were a wall to us both by night and by day, all the time we were with them tending the sheep. Now therefore, know and consider what you should do, for evil is plotted against our master and against all his household; and he is such a worthless man that no one can speak to him" (1 Samuel 25:14–17). The household certainly knew the lay of the land! Their frequent interactions with both the master and mistress led to their correct assessment of Nabal's foolishness and Abigail's wisdom. This was probably not the first time the servants had come to Abigail with a problem needing to be solved. The burden to save all their lives now rested on her slender shoulders. She quickly surmised what needed to be done after hearing the servants' report. Her husband had flagrantly insulted David and his men and she knew this could trigger swift retaliation. According to the servants' testimony, she also knew David and his men deserved generous compensation for their round-the-clock protection. Because the servants came to her, instead of Nabal, they showed their high regard for this great lady and full confidence in her decisions.

Abigail didn't fall apart or give in to panic when she heard the frightening news. Instead, she responded decisively and efficiently in this life-and-death emergency. She quickly gathered two hundred loaves of bread, two jugs of wine, five sheep already prepared to eat, nearly a bushel of roasted grain, one hundred clusters of raisins, and two hundred fig cakes. She packed them on donkeys and said to her servants, "Go on before me; behold, I am coming after you." But she didn't tell Nabal her plans (1 Samuel 25:18–19).

Her calculated decision and dangerous risk-taking certainly marked Abigail as a singular woman of great courage. Most women in her day would have never acted so forthrightly. "Abigail's initiative and independence were certainly rare for a married woman in the ancient Near East. In this case it was downright scandalous, since it entailed a clandestine meeting with one of her husband's enemies."[70]

Abigail, a gifted hands-on administrator, personally selected each food item. In those days, people would often send gifts on ahead of their arrival to meet someone, and all these provisions displayed extravagant generosity with a desire to appease. We may recall how Jacob sent loads of gifts on ahead of him to greet his estranged twin, Esau, to smooth the way (Genesis 32). Abigail was doing exactly what Nabal should have done but didn't. Of course, "this amount of food would not have been enough to feed six hundred men plus their families for any length of time, but it did represent a sizable token of appreciation and support for a fellow Judahite."[71]

"It came about as she was riding on her donkey and coming down by the hidden part of the mountain, that behold, David and his men were coming down toward her; so she met them" (1 Samuel 25:20). We can picture that scene! One lone woman facing David and four hundred incensed men bent on destruction! I admire everything about Abigail, especially her courage. Even more impressive was her singular willingness to save her household, including her foolish and cruel husband.

Right before they reached Abigail, David had been saying to his men, "Surely in vain I have guarded all that this man has in the wilderness, so that nothing was missed of all that belonged to him; and he has returned me evil for good. May God do so to the enemies of David, and more also, if by morning I leave as much as one male of any who belong to him" (1 Samuel 25:21–22). The text leaves no doubt as to David's dark intentions—to kill every man and boy belonging to Nabal's household as soon as he arrived in Maon.

The instant Abigail spotted David she quickly slid off her donkey and fell on her face before him, bowing low to the ground (1 Samuel 25:23). Before she uttered a single word, she let her body language speak for her. We can imagine David's astonishment as this beautiful, female apparition seemingly appeared out of nowhere to pay homage to him.

Once Abigail held David's undivided attention, she said, "On me alone, my lord, be the blame. And please let your maidservant speak to you, and listen to the words of your maidservant" (1 Samuel 25:24). She may have had more material possessions than David at that time, and she may have been mistress of a large household, but she assumed the role of a servant by placing herself under David and calling him her lord. And then, she altruistically accepted the blame for her husband's evil actions! David and his men had been focused on killing all the males, and the abrupt appearance of this beautiful woman stopped them in their tracks. Scripture doesn't mention Abigail's age when she confronted David and delivered the longest recorded speech by a woman in the Old Testament.[72] But, after reading her words, it further demonstrates why she was called both beautiful and wise! She entreated:

"Please do not let my lord pay attention to this worthless man, Nabal, for as his name is, so is he. Nabal is his name and folly is with him; but I your maidservant did not see the young men of my lord whom you sent. Now therefore, my lord, as the Lord lives, and as your soul lives, since the Lord has restrained you from shedding blood, and from avenging yourself by your own hand, now then let your enemies and those who seek evil against my lord, be as Nabal. Now let this gift, which your maidservant has brought to my lord be given to the young men who accompany my lord. Please forgive the transgression of your maidservant; for the Lord will certainly make for my lord an enduring house, because my lord is fighting the battles of the Lord, and evil will not be found in you all your days. Should anyone rise up to pursue you and to seek your life, then the life of my lord shall be bound in the bundle of the living with the Lord your God; but the lives of your enemies He will sling out as from the hollow of a sling. And when the Lord does for my lord according to all the good that He has spoken concerning you, and appoints you ruler over Israel, this will not cause grief or a troubled heart to my lord, both by having shed blood without cause and by my lord having avenged himself. When the Lord deals well with my lord, then remember your maidservant" (1 Samuel 25:25–31).

Abigail prefaced her speech by fully acknowledging her husband to be a wicked and ill-tempered fool and therefore, undeserving of any respect or credence. She distanced herself from her husband's response by saying she never even saw the men David had sent. Had she been able to intercept them, perhaps disaster could have been averted. She would have gladly fulfilled David's request as conveyed by his ten men.

Further, Abigail confidently assumed that her interruption of his mission would keep David from taking vengeance into his own hands by committing murder. She admitted her husband was a cursed man. She didn't try to sugarcoat him or make excuses for his reprehensible behavior. According to the culture of her day, she came bearing generous gifts for David and his men. She asked David to forgive her even though she had done nothing wrong! She knew God would reward David with a lasting dynasty if he allowed God to fight his battles for him. She acknowledged David's fugitive status and assured him of God's continued protection. She brilliantly alluded to his previous battle with Goliath and his divine deliverance, reminding him of God's favored protection as one who belonged to Him.

She prophetically asked him to peer into his future and consider that his current plan would leave a permanent blemish on his future role as Israel's king. She emphasized the benefits of a clear conscience. She obviously knew her God because she referred to Him seven times in her encounter with David and his men. Interestingly, Abigail called David "my lord" fourteen times in her lengthy speech. Since this Hebrew word also means "my husband,"[73] she would have addressed Nabal in similar fashion.

David listened to her impassioned, yet gentle speech, without interrupting. What a great courtesy to her! Then he responded, "'Blessed be the Lord God of Israel, who sent you this day to meet me, and blessed be your discernment, and blessed be you, who have kept me this day from bloodshed and from avenging myself by my own hand. Nevertheless, as the Lord God of Israel lives, who has restrained me from harming you, unless you had come quickly to meet me, surely there would not have been left to Nabal until the morning light as much as one male.' So David received from her hand what she had brought him and said to her, 'Go up to your house in peace. See, I have listened to you and granted your request'" (1 Samuel 25:32–35).

How wonderful that David first gave praise and glory to God, recognizing the spirit in which Abigail's speech was given. Even on the warpath, he remained cognizant of God's involvement in his life. David realized that God had sent Abigail to intervene and prevent bloodshed. David praised Abigail for her wisdom, blessing her quick actions and astute discernment. In a culture where women were often regarded as second-class citizens, this concession on David's part confirming his realization that she had been sent by God, simultaneously credited Abigail's courageous wisdom and elevated her as someone worthy of respect. So, David and his men turned around to head back to camp and Abigail headed for home. The fact that David completely reversed his course, abandoning his murderous plans, showed his change of heart and willingness to leave vengeance in God's hands, where it always belongs.

Abigail must have entertained so many different emotions as she rode her donkey back home: full of praise to her Lord, humbly grateful for how God had used her in such a big way, thrilled at seeing and interacting with the future king of Israel. Abigail had just conversed with the one of the biggest celebrities in the land, perhaps leaving her more than a little awestruck. And then she realized she was almost home and it was down to earth and back to the sad reality of her life.

Sure enough, she had not even been missed! Upon arrival, Abigail discovered Nabal throwing a big party and celebrating like a king. He was very drunk, so she didn't tell him anything about her meeting with David until dawn the next day. Nabal was too inebriated and self-absorbed to notice any missing food, let alone a missing wife! (1 Samuel 25:36). Something momentous had happened to her and she couldn't even share it with him. Nabal remained blatantly unaware of just how close he came to dying that night. His wife knew. The servants knew. Yet he ate and drank and partied as if he didn't have a care in the world.

It was probably a short and restless night for Abigail as she once again prepared to confront a man with a speech. She would have known from experience the best way to craft her words and deliver them to this cruel and foolish husband of hers. Perhaps she had to steel herself in preparation for a possibly volatile reaction from Nabal's response to her speech. "In the morning, when the wine had gone out of Nabal, his wife told him these things, and his heart died within him so that he became as a stone. About ten days later, the

Lord struck Nabal and he died" (1 Samuel 25:37–38). Apparently, Nabal's heart attack or massive stroke rendered him unable to even respond to his wife's report, which was a good thing! Earlier, Abigail had risked her life to save her husband's. Did she rush to his aid when he collapsed? Did she scream for the servants? Was she filled with awe, and perhaps relief, at this obviously divine disabling of her cruel husband? Whatever her reaction, we can be confident that her response to this unforeseen event reflected her heart of wisdom and compassion. Abigail's strong presence and solid decision-making ability would have helped comfort and direct the shaken servants.

Nabal lived for about ten more days before he died. The house must have seemed so quiet and peaceful without his disruptive and demanding presence. One of my friends endured marriage to a man prone to angry outbursts and harsh criticism. Whenever I visited their home, peace and quiet were elusive elements. When this man passed away, my friend's tense body relaxed and her facial features softened. No longer on guard, she blossomed into the woman she could have been had her husband cherished her and dealt tenderly with her. After a year as a widow, my friend married a wonderful man who loved her unconditionally, and eloquently expressed his love in word and deed almost daily. I wonder if Abigail felt the same relief that my friend did when her husband died?

"When David heard that Nabal was dead, he said, 'blessed be the Lord, who has pleaded the cause of my reproach from the hand of Nabal and has kept back His servant from evil. The Lord has also returned the evildoing of Nabal on his own head.' Then David sent a proposal to Abigail, to take her as his wife. When the servants of David came to Abigail at Carmel, they spoke to her, saying, 'David has sent us to you to take you as his wife'" (1 Samuel 25:39–40). "This marriage was important to David both materially (she was a wealthy widow), and politically. He came to have a marriage bond with an area that Saul had never effectively incorporated in his kingdom."[74]

We can only imagine Abigail's great joy at this wonderfully unexpected news! Her first marriage had been a nightmare. Divine release from its painful bonds allowed Abigail to experience a happy marriage with a handsome hunk destined to be king! I love her response to this marriage proposal! Abigail bowed low "with her face to the ground and said, 'Behold, your maidservant is a maid to wash the feet of my lord's servants.' Then Abigail quickly arose, and rode on a donkey, with her five maidens who attended her; and she followed the messengers of David and became his wife" (1 Samuel 25:41–42).

This beautiful woman continued to be pleasing to God and others with her righteous actions and humble attitude. Even though she joined David, bringing her own attending servants, she still relegated herself to a lowly servant position. We marvel at this sweet woman's depth of humility, even being willing to wash the feet of David's servants. She gladly left a life of luxury cognizant of the rough life that lay ahead. As fugitives, they would constantly be on the run, scrambling for food, clothing, and shelter. Joining her life to David's would place her in constant jeopardy. Despite all this, she consented to marrying her "Prince Charming," and future king of Israel. David began his reign at age thirty (2 Samuel 5:4), so he was in his twenties when he married Abigail.

Soon after their marriage, Abigail's new husband had another altercation with a pursuing King Saul (1 Samuel 26). In David's encounter with Saul, Abigail could be proud of her husband who acted righteously, instead of taking vengeance into his own hands. Perhaps David's recent experience with Nabal helped him realize the Lord would fight his battles. Earlier, David had sworn a solemn oath to Abigail that he would not harm her or Nabal. Now, presented with an opportunity to kill Saul, David once more enacted the same oath, refraining from killing the Lord's annointed, even though his fighting companion, Abishai, encouraged him to do so. Instead, David, perhaps recalling how Nabal died, told his fellow-warrior, "As the Lord lives, surely the Lord will strike him, or his day will come that he dies, or he will go down into battle and perish" (1 Samuel 26:10). With Abigail's sweet reminder, David had learned a valuable lifelong lesson—to allow the Lord fight his battles for him.

After this tense encounter with Saul, David decided to move his family, and the families of all his warriors, into the enemy territory of the Philistines, figuring Saul would not so easily pursue him there. After David worked hard to earn the trust of the Philistine monarch, he requested the king's permission to move his large entourage into a village in the country. For over a year, David and Abigail, along with all in their company, made the town of Ziklag their home. Living in enemy territory did not deter David from carrying out clandestine raids against the Philistines. Perhaps Abigail worried about her husband's dangerous missions and warned him to be careful. David cleverly played the double-agent role to such a sophisticated degree that the Philistine king believed David had fully aligned his allegiance with him and had completely alienated his own people in Israel (1 Samuel 27).

David may have fooled the Philistine king, but the king's men were another story. As David and his warriors played their part by joining the Philistine army to make a raid on Israel, the Philistine lords made such a stink that the king said to David, "I know that you are pleasing in my sight, like an angel of God; nevertheless, the commanders of the Philistines have said, 'He must not go up with us to battle'" (1 Samuel 29:10). David's bluff had been called, but by God's divine providence he was able to remain in the king's good graces.

As David and his men began the three-day trek back home to their families in Ziklag, they had no idea disaster awaited them. While they had been collaborating with the Philistine enemy, another enemy, the Amalekites, had raided Ziklag and burned it with fire, taking captive all the women and children. What must that have been like for Abigail and the others, so defenseless without their mighty fighting men? We know what it was like for David and all his men when they witnessed the horrific destruction of Ziklag and the absence of their precious families. They "lifted their voices and wept until there was no strength in them to weep" (1 Samuel 30:4). Not knowing where their loved ones were, whether they were alive or dead, would have been excruciating.

Once the initial outpouring of grief subsided, David's men, incensed with anger, unleashed it on David, blaming him. "Moreover David was greatly distressed because the people spoke of stoning him, for all the people were embittered, each one because of his sons and his daughters. But David strengthened himself in the Lord his God" (1 Samuel 30:6). The best leaders are those whose strength is sourced in God and in the power of His word. "David inquired of the Lord, saying, 'Shall I pursue this band? Shall I overtake them?' And He said to him, 'Pursue, for you will surely overtake then, and you will surely rescue all'" (1 Samuel 30:8). Abigail could not have married two more different men. Given devastating news, Abigail's first husband, Nabal, suffered a massive stroke. He had no strength outside of himself upon which to rely. David's dependence upon God made him stronger, not weaker, in this horrific crisis.

As David and four hundred of his mighty men set out in hot pursuit, God led them to a young Egyptian boy, weak and sick, who had been part of the Amalekite raid on Ziklag. He had been left behind to die. After David provided water and some food, this young boy rallied enough to lead them to the Amalekite camp. While the enemy partied in celebration, David launched a surprise attack, overcoming them and rescuing everyone. Providentially, nothing was missing and no one was hurt (1 Samuel 30). David, Abigail's heroic husband, had rescued her twice—once from Nabal and now from the Amalekites.

After the death of King Saul and his sons (1 Samuel 31), God told David to move his family back into Israel to the town of Hebron where David would reign over Judah for seven and one half years. It was here in the town of Hebron that God allowed Abigail to conceive and give birth to a son whom she named Chileab, which means *like his father* [75] (2 Samuel 3:1–3). Perhaps the name intentionally carried the hope that her little boy would grow up to emulate his father in physical and spiritual ways. Given her painful history with Nabal, Abigail, one of David's eight wives, perhaps had the greatest appreciation for him as a husband and father. Certainly, David embodied the antithesis of Nabal. We can expect that Abigail demonstrated her love and respect for David in multiple, tangible ways throughout her marriage to him.

Abigail not only pleased David, but more importantly she pleased God. Like Abigail, all of us make choices every day to please God, please others, or please ourselves. I'm very convicted when I notice that there is not one single time where she chose to please herself. She was all about pleasing God and others, often at great sacrifice to herself.

After reading about her remarkable life, we know Abigail was not faking it. She was the real deal. Have you ever, like me, sat in class and heard the dreaded words, "pop quiz"? There is no time to study or cram for this surprise test. The purpose of a pop quiz is to ascertain what we already know about a given subject and to assess if we've been paying attention in class. Pop quizzes carry over into real life as well. Whenever we are faced with a situation that surprises us and requires a quick response, what's inside comes out. How much of God's Word have we internalized and are able to apply to our test?

As a little girl, my friends and I enjoyed playing with paper dolls and designing clothes for them. These flat one-dimensional figures filled many a rainy day with creative fun for us. Thankfully, God didn't make us like paper dolls. We are three-dimensional beings made up of mind, emotion, and will. By studying how Abigail responded to her pop quizzes, we can see her mind, emotions, and will operating together to produce a holistic and positive response. In reading her story, we can plainly see how her pop quiz results pleased God. So how can we, like Abigail, define our ambition, determine our actions, and direct our attitudes in ways that please God? Let's examine three ways, each with three verses to consider and three questions to answer, helping us apply God's truth to our lives.

Defining our Ambition

It's clear from Abigail's speech to David that she made it her ambition to know God. Her knowledge of Him led to her desire to please Him. We marvel at everything Abigail said about God in her speech. She acknowledged His existence, His eternality, His sovereignty, His blessing, His protection, His plans for the future, and His faithfulness. If we desire to know God the way Abigail did, we need to make it our ambition to pursue Him through studying His Word. As believers on this side of the cross, we have the precious gift of the indwelling Holy Spirit, enabling us to know the mind of Christ as we study the Scriptures and apply God's truth to govern our words and actions. There's not one recorded thing Abigail did or said that contradicted God and His Word. That's impressive and inspiring! Let's look at three supporting verses for defining our ambition:

"We also have as our ambition, whether at home [living here on earth], or absent [gone from this earth and at Home in heaven], to be pleasing to Him" (2 Corinthians 5:9).

To have an ambition automatically entails hard work. It will not always be easy to make the choice to please God. It may prevent us from accepting a certain job, or from going to a certain party, or any number of things that comprise life here on earth. When we get serious about pleasing God in everything, it makes us ask the hard questions and then submit to the right answers. We can never go wrong in pleasing God if we know and obey His Word, and are receptively obedient to the Spirit's leading.

"Let love be your highest goal!" (1 Corinthians 14:1, NLT).

This verse follows the famous love chapter of 1 Corinthians 13. We may be familiar with Elisabeth Barrett Browning's poem, "How do I love thee? Let me count the ways." Well, 1 Corinthians 13 certainly counts the ways! After studying this passage, there is no doubt as to what love looks like, acts like, and accomplishes. At the end of this chapter, it's abundantly clear that love rules the day. That's why 1 Corinthians 14:1 reiterates the theme of love. When loving God and loving others becomes our highest goal, we are sure to please Him.

"If pleasing people were my goal, I would not be Christ's servant" (Galatians 1:10, NLT).

From whom do we seek approval: from God or from people? When we answer that question honestly, it helps us define our ambition, which in turn guides our motives. Paul, in calling himself "Christ's servant," declared his allegiance. The goal of pleasing God superseded pleasing others. We often think of a servant as occupying a degrading position complete with drudgery and unrewarded toil. But one writer helps shed a different light. "Undoubtedly the background for the concept of being the Lord's slave or servant is to be found in the Old Testament Scriptures. For a Jew, this concept did not connote drudgery, but honor and privilege. It was used of national Israel at times (Isaiah 43:10), but was especially associated with famous Old Testament personalities, including such great men as Moses (Joshua 14:7), David (Psalm 89:3; cf. 2 Samuel 7:5, 8), and Elijah (2 Kings 10:10); all these men were "servants (or slaves) of the Lord."[76] Given Abigail's humble willingness to serve David and even his servants, she easily qualifies as one worthy of being included in this list of exemplary men! Likewise, we should be willing to serve others, even those we would erroneously deem as "beneath" us. As followers of Jesus Christ, it is our highest honor and privilege to be known as one of His servants. Based on these verses, we can ask ourselves three questions:

- Am I seeking to please God in everything?
- Am I known for loving others?
- Is my highest goal to please people or please Jesus?

Determining our Actions

In examining Abigail's life, we can't help but notice that her sacrificial actions reflected her determination to be pleasing to God.

The moment Abigail heard about Nabal's selfish rebuttal and the servants' warning that evil was plotted against the master, she sprang into action and rushed to gather provisions from her pantry. Then she courageously set out to intercept David. Throughout this tense drama, Abigail's actions never contradicted her knowledge of God; instead she received high praise from David when he told her, "Blessed be the Lord God of Israel, who sent you this day to meet me and blessed be your discernment, and blessed be you, who have kept me this day from bloodshed and from avenging myself by my own hand!" (1 Samuel 25:32–33). Abigail risked her life to save others. She courageously faced the prospect of suffering and pain to please God. Let's look at three supporting verses for determining our actions:

"Oh that my actions would consistently reflect your decrees!" (Psalm 119:5, NLT).

The NET Bible translates verse 5, "If only I were predisposed to keep your statutes!" Isn't that the truth? More often than I want to admit, my actions fail to reflect God's Word because I'm so strongly predisposed to pleasing myself first! Given my fallen human nature, my first response to any situation often reveals my selfish heart and strong desire to make me, not God, look good. However, when our right response to circumstances reflects God's truth, we impact others in powerfully God-glorifying ways as we put His Word into practice with our obedient actions.

"Commit your actions to the Lord and your plans will succeed" (Proverbs 16:3, NLT).

The verse right before this one says, "All a person's ways seem right in his own opinion, but the Lord evaluates the motives" (Proverbs 16:2, NET). That's why I need to be completely dependent upon the Holy Spirit's guidance. I may do the right thing but with the wrong motives. I can find myself wanting others to notice and approve my actions, which is prideful and self-promoting. All too often, I'm more concerned about looking good for the sake of receiving praise from others, rather than wanting all the praise to go to God alone. Proverbs 27:21 is a great reminder that, "Fire tests the purity of silver and gold, but a person is tested by being praised" (NLT). I'm trying to learn to deflect any praise I receive by quickly redirecting it to the One deserving of all praise. I can't make any of my plans succeed in the sense of counting for eternity, only God can. Without God's approval and guidance, my plans are like paper dolls dissolving in the rain.

> *"Our actions will show that we belong to the truth, so we will be confident when we stand before God"* (1 John 3:19, NLT).

In the preceding verse John cautions, "Little children, let us not love with word or with tongue but in deed and truth (1 John 3:18, NET). Our actions can validate or negate our words. Words can be cheap while actions are costlier. We can easily say what we don't really mean! Or we can promise something we know we'll never fulfill. According to Romans 14:12, "each of us will give a personal account to God" (NLT). Our actions today matter tomorrow because our God is watching and evaluating whether or not we are walking in the light and truth of His Word. When our actions are based on God's decrees, we can be confident instead of cowering, when the time comes to stand before Him to give an account. Based on these verses, we can ask ourselves three questions:

- Do my actions reflect my obedience to God's Word?
- Have I committed all my plans to God and will they please Him?
- Will my actions commend or embarrass me when I stand before God one day?

Directing our Attitudes

I marvel at Abigail's attitude considering her circumstances. She wasn't bitter, angry, vindictive, or self-pitying. Honestly, I'm afraid that I would have blurted out the truth of Nabal's narrow escape at his big party where everyone could hear how foolishly he had acted. I also wonder if I would have gone out of my way to risk my life to save Nabal's. It would have been so easy to just let David kill him and be freed from a miserable marriage. But Abigail knew that would not please her God. I'm also impressed with Abigail's attitude of selfless humility. Time and again we see her bowing low before others—even David's servants! She emptied herself of any self-gratifying or self-glorifying ambitions, choosing to think and act like a humble servant, which is truly inspiring!

Jesus emptied Himself of His right to visibly display all His splendor and glory to please and serve Himself.[77] He could have performed countless self-serving miracles. Instead, His miracles ministered to others and glorified the Father. Jesus chose to humbly serve the creatures He had created instead of forcing them to serve Him. Let's look at three supporting verses for directing our attitudes:

"For the kingdom of God is not a matter of eating and drinking, but of righteousness, peace and joy in the Holy Spirit, because anyone who serves Christ in this way is pleasing to God and receives human approval. So then, we pursue the things that make for peace and the building up of one another" (Romans 14:17–19, NIV).

In the context surrounding these verses, some early Christians were placing too much emphasis on external practices instead of concentrating on making sure their lives reflected peace and joy in the Holy Spirit. They were getting all hung up on the technicalities of whether to eat the meat sold in the marketplace that had previously been offered to false idols in pagan temples. The Apostle Paul knew that those who chose to eat only vegetables, because they thought eating meat offered to idols made them complicit in the pagan practice, would be tempted to judge other believers for not doing the same. Paul also knew that those who believed they could eat anything offered to idols because of their freedom in Christ could be tempted to judge those who restricted their diets. Entertaining a judgmental and critical attitude toward others only causes disunity, which is not pleasing to God. That's why Paul urged both sides, "So then, we pursue the things which make for peace and the building up of one another" (Romans 14:19).

"All of you be harmonious, sympathetic, affectionate, compassionate, and humble" (1 Peter 3:8, NET).

The immediate context of 1 Peter 3 refers to the husband/wife relationship, but the principles apply to believers' relationships with others as well. Let's take a brief look at each characteristic mentioned in this verse: To be ***harmonious*** has the idea of being musically pleasing. Whenever I hear a modern piece of classical music emphasizing discordant arrangements, my nerves feel on edge rather than calmed. I may be considered unsophisticated in this regard, but I can find no redeeming beauty in all the dissonance! Personally, I love the romantic classical compositions full of sweeping melodious chords. In these pieces, even when a variety of instruments are playing different notes, they all harmonize beautifully with each other. Likewise, in the body of Christ members have different gifts, but when played together according to Christ's notes, produce harmony in the church. Sometimes I wonder if our discordant interactions with others sound like horrible music to God's ears! It most certainly could not be called music to my ears when my own children were loudly at odds with each other!

To be ***sympathetic*** entails being sensitive to the needs of others. Being sensitive requires less preoccupation with self and more awareness of how we can best minister to others. Biblically speaking, it's putting others' concerns before our own. "Be devoted to one another in brotherly love; give preference to one another in honor" (Romans 12:10). A heartfelt hug and a simple, "I'm so sorry!" can go far in expressing our sympathy. Another way to show sympathy is to simply listen to others as they pour out their pain to us. It's helpful to resist the urge we feel to interrupt them, give advice, or jump in with our own story of suffering. Someone who can just listen with complete attention, and then lovingly express sympathy, acts like a healing salve soothing a painful wound.

To be ***affectionate*** is to express our love for each other. It's a good thing to feel affection for another believer, but even better to show it with actions that clearly demonstrate the love we feel for them. It blesses all who observe our affection in action. I suffered from a chronic condition in my teens and twenties. My ovaries periodically grew grapefruit-sized cysts that eventually burst, often requiring immediate surgery. I lost one ovary two years after the birth of our first child and despite ongoing ovarian issues, God allowed me to conceive again. However, my gynecologist warned me that the next huge cyst might compromise my remaining ovary to such a degree that I would most likely lose it. Sure enough, when our second son was only ten months old, my body grew another cyst and with that surgery I lost my second ovary, as well as my other reproductive equipment. Undergoing a complete hysterectomy at age thirty was very traumatic to say the least! After surgery, I went through a time of grieving, emotional upheaval, and physical exhaustion. But I experienced affection in action as my church body rallied around to provide meals, housecleaning, and babysitting for three months. During my recuperation, my sweet husband would come home after a long day of teaching to take over childcare and housework duties. This sacrificial ministering demonstrated the love of Christ, as fellow believers became His hands and His feet to humbly serve me.

To be **compassionate** displays our tenderhearted concern for others. When a catastrophe or distressing circumstance arises in another's life, a compassionate attitude can minister deeply. However, it can cost us to show compassion toward others. It requires removing the focus of attention away from us and onto others. It takes time and effort to notice the needs and concerns of others. It sometimes necessitates our sacrificial love to help meet their needs as we turn our intentions into actions. But what a beautiful gift to give to others!

To be **humble** is to view ourselves from God's perspective. We are simply sinners saved by grace alone, through faith alone, in Christ alone. We are nothing without Him. Humility is a rare quality these days in our culture of self-absorption and self-promotion! Humility begins on the inside as an attitude of the heart. You've seen those performers on stage who pretend to deflect applause while at the same time motioning with their hands for it to continue. We do the same thing sometimes with compliments directed our way because we have such an insatiable need for recognition and affirmation from others. Learning humility requires a lifetime of submitting ourselves to God and putting others' needs above our own. As believers, we know how much God blesses a humble heart. We can never go wrong in following the supreme example of Jesus who continually humbled Himself in myriad ways when He walked this earth. We can observe a common thread running through all these attributes. They begin as attitudes resulting in actions that bless and please all who observe them—especially God!

"Devote yourselves to prayer, keeping alert in it with an attitude of thanksgiving" (Colossians 4:2).

Why is an attitude of gratitude so crucial and transformational? When we have a prevailing mindset of thankfulness, we see everything through a lens of gratitude to our God. Earlier in this book, Paul wrote, "Just as you received Christ Jesus as Lord, continue to live your lives in him, rooted and built up in him and firm in your faith just as you were taught, and overflowing with thankfulness" (Colossians 2:6–7, NET). If we are overflowing with thankfulness, we are maintaining an attitude of gratitude in everything and for everything. Later, in chapter 3 verse 15, we are told to "Let the peace of Christ be in control in your heart, and be thankful" (NET). Finally, in verse 17 we read, "Whatever you do in word or deed, do it all in the name of the Lord Jesus, giving thanks to God the Father through him" (NET). That pretty much covers it! Whatever we're doing, whatever we're saying, whatever we're feeling, we're supposed to be displaying an attitude of gratitude to our God.

It's a worthy endeavor to develop the habit of finding at least three things to be thankful for in every adverse situation. This goes a long way to offset the negative and accentuate the positive. I fall way short of this admonition most of the time, but because I'm commanded to be thankful, I know that it's possible with God's help to be continually grateful. Based on these verses, we can ask ourselves three questions:

- What is my pervasive attitude? Am I judgmental or am I reflecting goodness, peace, and joy in the Holy Spirit?
- Am I being harmonious, sympathetic, affectionate, compassionate, and humble with others?
- Am I praying for everything with a thankful heart?

We began our application section with 2 Corinthians 5:9. "We have as our ambition, whether at home or absent, to be pleasing to Him." I want to end with 2 Corinthians 5:10. "For we must all appear before the judgment seat of Christ, so that each one may be recompensed for his deeds in the body, according to what he has done, whether good or bad."

The fact that "we must all appear," guarantees a divine appointment we can't wiggle out of by canceling. Sometimes, I've rescheduled a doctor's or dentist's appointment on my calendar simply because I didn't feel like going that day. I can't reschedule or cancel my future appointment with Jesus. One day, I will have to stand before Him as my works are evaluated. I will then be rewarded or not rewarded for everything I've done as a believer in Jesus here on earth.

One writer helps us understand the phrase, "whether good or bad" when he explains, "The Greek word translated 'bad' (*phaulos*) really means worthless. The idea is not that God will reward us for the good things we did and punish us for the bad things we did. He will rather reward us for the worthwhile things we did and not reward us for the worthless things we did (cf. Matthew 6:19–21; 1 Corinthians 9:24–27). The worthwhile things are those that contribute to the advancement of God's mission and glory in the world. Worthless deeds are those that make no contribution to the fulfillment of God's good purposes (cf. Matthew 25:14–30; Luke 19:11–27)."[78]

Just as we appreciate a professor telling us what areas will be covered on an upcoming exam, it's especially helpful to know some of what Christ will examine at the judgment seat. Thankfully, Scripture gives us the test questions so we can be preparing for it in this life. "Here are some of the main areas that will be examined when we stand before the Lord:

1. How we treat other believers (Matthew 10:41–42; Hebrews 6:10).

2. How we employ our God-given talents, abilities, and opportunities (Matthew 25:14–29; Luke 19:11–26; 1 Corinthians 12:4, 7; 2 Timothy 1:6; 1 Peter 4:10).

3. How we use our money (Matthew 6:1–4; 1 Timothy 6:17–19).

4. How well we endure personal injustice and being mistreated (Matthew 5:11–12; Mark 10:29–30; Luke 6:27–28, 35; Romans 8:18; 2 Corinthians 4:17; 1 Peter 4:12–13).

5. How we endure suffering and trials (James 1:12; Revelation 2:10).

6. How we spend our time (Psalm 90:9–12; Ephesians 5:15–16; Colossians 4:5; 1 Peter 1:17).

7. How we run the God-designed race He has mapped out for us (1 Corinthians 9:24; Philippians 2:16; 3:12–14; Hebrews 12:1).

8. How effectively we control our fleshly appetites (1 Corinthians 9:25–27; Romans 16:18).

9. How many souls we witness to and win for Christ (Daniel 12:3; 1 Thessalonians 2:19–20).

10. How much we are looking forward to His return (2 Timothy 4:8).

11. How devoted we are to God's Word and God's people (2 Timothy 4:2; Romans 12:10).

12. How humble we are (Matthew 18:1–6).

13. How hospitable we are (1 Peter 4:9)

14. How faithful we are in our vocation (Colossians 3:23–24).

15. How well we govern our words (Matthew 12:36–37)."[79]

Reflecting on this coming event, Romans 8:1 is so reassuring, "There is now **no** condemnation for those who are in Christ Jesus." Praise God we stand forgiven and righteous in His sight! As believers, we are in Jesus and covered by His righteousness (Philippians 3:9). Since God sees us as already righteous in Christ, we know we will **not** be judged or condemned for our sins because Jesus paid the penalty of death that sin demands by dying on the cross in our place. His sacrifice freed us from eternal condemnation. That's cause for eternal gratitude! Just to be crystal clear: our salvation is based on Christ's perfect work. Rewards are based on our works for Christ as empowered by the Holy Spirit.

Just knowing I have a divine appointment already on the books makes me want to be a 2 Corinthians 5:9 follower of Christ because 2 Corinthians 5:10 is coming! Since Jesus knows and evaluates the motives behind all our work for Him, He is the perfect Judge, so His rewards will be perfectly just. We can take comfort in this truth and we can also find motivation to live the rest of our lives focused on pleasing Him. May I encourage you with one final verse from Philippians? Just in case you think pleasing God is all up to you and dependent upon your own efforts, that couldn't be further from the truth! "For God is working in you, giving you the desire and the power to do what pleases Him" (Philippians 2:13, NET).

Abigail certainly pleased God in multiple ways as she dealt with her servants, as she gathered gifts for David and his men, as she humbly confronted David and his warriors with God-honoring words, and as she willingly stepped into David's life as his wife. As she lived her life to please others in altruistic, rather than self-serving ways, she must have brought great joy to all who were privileged to know her. The name Abigail means *the father's joy* or *my father rejoices*.[80] I want to bring a smile to my heavenly Father's face by being pleasing to Him, just like Abigail. My prayer for us is that we will make it our mission in life to be pleasing to God. We'll be eternally grateful that we did!

Father God, thank You for giving us such a great example in Abigail and an even greater example in Jesus. May we define our ambition, determine our actions, and direct our attitudes in ways that please You. Thank You for the wonderful assurance that You are working in us all the time, giving us the desire and the power to please You. May our coming appointment before the judgment seat of Christ motivate us to please You as we look forward to receiving rewards we can use to worship You. I pray You would enable us to live grateful lives of humble service that will count for eternity. In the name of the One who pleases You the most, we pray, Amen.

Focus Points

1. Did you learn anything new about Abigail? In what ways do you identify with her?

2. Using the following scale, rate yourself on these questions taken from each application point:

   Hardly ever   Not often enough   Most of the time
   - Is pleasing God the motivation behind what I do and say?
   - Would my family members describe me as loving?
   - Am I more concerned with pleasing Jesus or pleasing myself?
   - Am I obedient or disobedient to Scripture in what I do and say?
   - Do I commit my plans to God and will these plans please Him?
   - When I think about my past week, will what I have done commend or embarrass me when I stand before God someday?
   - What is my pervasive attitude? Am I judgmental or am I reflecting goodness, peace, and joy in the Holy Spirit?
   - Am I being harmonious, sympathetic, affectionate, compassionate and humble with others, especially those closest to me?
   - Do my prayers reflect a thankful heart?

3. Based on how you honestly answered these nine questions from this chapter, choose one to focus on this week. Please do not let these questions discourage you! All of us are works in progress as God continues to transform us into Christlikeness.

4. As you read the following verses, select an aspect from each one that you can focus on this week in your quest to be pleasing to Him. The first verse is completed as an example:
Psalm 104:34 – what I think about
Proverbs 15:8
Romans 15:1–2
Ephesians 5:8–10
Colossians 1:9–12
1 Timothy 2:1–3
Hebrews 11:6
Hebrews 13:15–16
1 John 3:21–22

5. Finally, review the set of test questions regarding our upcoming appointment with Jesus at the Judgment Seat of Christ. Then, choose one or more to focus on as you ask God to help you be more faithful and purposeful in that area of your life.

IV

Bathsheba: Finding Forgiveness

Is there someone in your circle of family and friends whom you are having a hard time forgiving? Has someone offended you and failed to ask you to forgive them? If so, are you having a hard time moving on with your life because you're waiting for an apology? Have you ever struggled with forgiving yourself, even when you know God has forgiven you? Do you wrestle with the difference between forgiving and forgetting? How's that for asking the hard questions right up front!

Forgiving is never a one-time action, it is always ongoing because life is messy and relationships are often difficult to navigate. People will inevitably hurt us, misunderstand us, and disappoint us. I think of one such woman in Scripture who was terribly hurt and deeply disappointed when a man's lust for her resulted in the murder of her husband and the loss of her child. As we uncover her story, we will see God's forgiveness washing over all the ugliness as His mercy and grace win the day. We will also further explore the topic of forgiveness and its daily necessity in our lives by addressing our opening questions.

We first meet Bathsheba in 2 Samuel 11. "Then it happened in the spring, at the time when kings go out to battle, that David sent Joab and his servants with him and all Israel, and they destroyed the sons of Ammon and besieged Rabbah. But David stayed at Jerusalem" (2 Samuel 11:1). The Ammonites were a people group who had their origins in the incestuous encounter between Lot and his younger daughter (Genesis 19:37–38). During King Saul's reign, Israel defeated the Ammonites and forced them into servitude (1 Samuel 11). King David continued Israel's sovereignty over this hostile people group by besieging their capital city to defeat them again. The Ammonites were excluded from entering the assembly of the Lord because they refused to let Israel pass through their land when the beleaguered Israelites, released from bondage in Egypt, journeyed to inhabit a new land promised them by God (Deuteronomy 23:3–4).

Spring typically signals an end to the rainy season in the Middle East making it a logistically practical time to engage in war. Horse hooves and chariot wheels don't get so bogged down in sticky mud. We're not told why David chose to stay at home for this battle. We do know from another incidence in 2 Samuel 21:17, that his men strongly advised him to remain in Jerusalem out of harm's way. They did not want to see the "lamp of Israel" extinguished. Perhaps he had been counseled by his advisors to sit this war out as well.

One evening, with his men away, fighting for his kingdom, "David arose from his bed and walked around on the roof of the king's house, and from his roof he saw a woman bathing; and the woman was very beautiful in appearance" (2 Samuel 11:2). Perhaps this man of action, accustomed to the danger and adrenalin-laced atmosphere of battle, faced boredom and sought some visual excitement for entertainment. It wasn't like he didn't have ample female companionship at his disposal in the form of wives and concubines. However, as he fixated on this bathing beauty, "David sent and inquired about the woman.

And one said, 'Is this not Bathsheba, the daughter of Eliam, the wife of Uriah the Hittite?'" (2 Samuel 11:3).

Bathsheba's house must have been close enough to the palace rooftop for David to notice her alluring beauty and his eyes lingered as he watched her bathe her body. From the high vantage point of his palace rooftop, David could view any number of roofs below him. In Bathsheba's day, many activities took place on the flat-roofed house-tops, including bathing, where it could be cooler. Some years ago, my husband, Mark, and I stayed at a friend's home nestled in the crowded hills of the Bay Area in northern California. With property at a premium, the lots weren't just zero, they were sub-zero! As we stepped out onto the patio early one evening, we immediately noticed the lack of privacy for everyone below us. Their decks and yards lay fully exposed before our eyes. Scripture does not say if Bathsheba knew David could see her and therefore set out to entrap him; or if she was completely unaware she had an audience. Since we're not told, I don't think we can presume to judge her motives.

Who was this beautiful woman? Her name means *seventh daughter* and can also be translated *daughter of the oath*.[81] Her grandfather, Ahithophel, was one of King David's closest advisors. Her father, Eliam, was a member of David's elite warrior group known as "the Thirty." These men enjoyed superhero status in the land due to their legendary bravery and mighty deeds. Her husband, Uriah, was also a member of this elite group, so she obviously came from a very prominent and well-connected family with close ties to the king (2 Samuel 23:8–39).

David looked long enough to lust and then gave birth to his lust, because he "sent some messengers to get her. She came to him, and he had sexual relations with her. (Now at that time she was in the process of purifying herself from her menstrual uncleanness)"

(2 Samuel 11:4, NET). James 1:14–15 describes exactly what happened to King David, and can happen to us, when we choose to engage in sin. "Temptation comes from our own desires, which entice us and drag us away. These desires give birth to sinful actions. And when sin is allowed to grow, it gives birth to death" (NLT). When the king yielded to his lustful desire for Bathsheba, he set into motion some catastrophic consequences that did indeed lead to death.

Spiritual battles are just as intense, if not more so, than physical ones. The king had not involved himself in the current war against the Ammonites, but the spiritual war he waged when he gazed lustfully at Bathsheba, turned his palace rooftop into a battlefield. Just as engaging in physical battle tests our strength, stamina, skill, and knowledge; the same arenas face intense scrutiny in spiritual warfare. Just as physical warfare requires armor and ammunition; spiritual battles do as well. In Ephesians 6:10–17, we find the believer's arsenal of armor and weaponry needed to wage war in the spiritual realm. We may be caught by surprise, but we never have to be caught defenseless.

Bathsheba would not have dared disobey a direct summons from the king. She had no choice but to be escorted by David's messengers into the palace. According to Leviticus 15:28, after a woman's menstrual discharge ceased, she needed to count off seven days and then go through her purification rites, which included bathing. Bathsheba would have just been starting her ovulation cycle when King David summoned her. Even though the king knew whose wife, daughter, and granddaughter she was, his desire for her obliterated all sound thought or reason. As king, David's harem awaited his attentions, but he wanted Bathsheba.

After having relations with her, David sent Bathsheba back to her house. You may be familiar with the term, "Walk of Shame," referring to someone who returns home after a one-night stand.[82] Often, the individual's appearance and clothing are disheveled as they walk home with head downcast. Bathsheba could relate to that. If Bathsheba had orchestrated her bathing to be seen by the king, then her motives would have been to entrap him and her night in the palace would have thrilled her. On the other hand, if Bathsheba remained unaware of her royal audience, her escort to the palace and intercourse with David constituted rape.

Envisioning ourselves in her place, we may ask some "I wonder" questions:

> Did she feel like taking another bath after she got home from her illicit encounter with David in the palace?
> Did she wrestle with guilt, pain, fear, and confusion?
> Was she angry with Uriah for leaving her alone and defenseless?
> If she had exposed her body hoping to attract David's attention, did it go farther than she intended?
> If she had indeed been raped, was she able to confess her dilemma to a close confidant and seek consolation and advice?
> How did she deal with the shock of her resultant pregnancy?

With the undeniable result of their encounter confirmed in her body, Bathsheba's two-word message to David must have rocked his world: "I'm pregnant" (2 Samuel 11:5). Apparently, Bathsheba was not a loose woman prone to sleeping around and cheating on her husband because when David heard the news, he instantly knew he was the father. He didn't try to blame anyone else. This inconvenient and upsetting news prompted David to try to cover up his sin as he came up with a plan to manipulate the situation to his advantage.

There were already several people who knew what had happened that night—the messengers who brought Bathsheba to the palace, as well as other servants. Word may have spread as juicy tidbits of royal gossip hit the streets. Responding to Bathsheba's surprise pregnancy, "David sent to Joab [Uriah's commander] saying, 'Send me Uriah the Hittite'" (2 Samuel 11:6). He had to be very specific here—he didn't want the wrong Uriah coming home! Uriah may have been of Hittite extraction, but his name seems to indicate an allegiance to David's God, Yahweh, as his name means *Yahweh is my light.*[83]

When Uriah arrived home from the battlefield, David cordially greeted him and asked him how the war was progressing. "Not knowing what urgent matter had necessitated this forty-plus-mile trip to Jerusalem, Uriah might have been somewhat surprised to find that the king merely wanted to know how the war was going. Such comparatively trivial information could have been acquired from any of the runners who kept David informed of the battle's progress—it certainly didn't need to come from one of the Thirty."[84]

Then the king commanded Uriah, "Go down to your house, and wash your feet" (2 Samuel 11: 8). Now to us that may sound strange. We may think his feet must have been disgustingly filthy. However, when read in Hebrew, another meaning can arise. "Given the euphemistic use of 'feet' in the sense of 'genitals,' David would thus be suggesting to Uriah that he 'enjoy his wife sexually.'"[85] David desperately wanted Uriah to go home to be with his wife so that his baby growing inside her could be passed off as Uriah's.

David's plan failed miserably when he learned that Uriah didn't go home after all. Instead he spent the night outside David's palace where his guards slept. Why did he disobey a direct order from his king? When David once again summoned him to ask why he didn't go home to be with his wife after being away so long, Uriah's reply revealed his righteous character. Bathsheba's husband explained that all the armies of Judah and Israel were living in tents and some were even sleeping in open fields. In addition, the ark of the covenant accompanied them on the battlefield. How could he possibly, in good conscience, go home and enjoy his wife when other soldiers could not enjoy the same privileges? (2 Samuel 11:9–11). Any war which included the presence of the ark of the covenant was deemed holy. If Uriah wanted to remain consecrated as he rejoined the battle, then he needed to abstain from sexual activity.[86]

Plan A fell apart, so David implemented Plan B. The king invited Uriah to dinner with the goal of getting him good and drunk. Then with inhibitions lowered, he hoped Uriah would go home to sleep with his wife. For the next two nights, even in a drunken stupor, Uriah refused to go home but once again slept outside the palace entrance (2 Samuel 11:12–13).

Desperate to resolve this situation and save face in the process, David conceived Plan C: orchestrate Uriah's murder. He wrote a letter to Joab to station Uriah on the front lines and then have everyone draw back, leaving him up front as an easy target. Uriah had no idea he was delivering his own death sentence to Joab when he took David's message back to the battlefield (2 Samuel 11:14–15).

We may wonder if Bathsheba even knew her husband, Uriah, was home from the war, being entertained by the king, and sleeping in the outer regions of the palace where the king's servants slept. It's not hard to wonder if some servant may have leaked the news to her. I also wonder if she struggled with morning sickness in this pregnancy. If she knew Uriah was in the vicinity, maybe she dreaded seeing him and perhaps felt relief that he left her alone. Or maybe she longed to pour out her troubles to him. Certainly, her emotions were uncomfortably conflicted.

David's Plan C succeeded. "So as Joab kept watch on the city, he stationed Uriah at the place where he knew the best enemy soldiers were. When the men of the city came out and fought with Joab, some of David's soldiers fell in battle. Uriah the Hittite also died" (2 Samuel 11:16–17, NET). Tragically, David's attempt to cover up his sin resulted in death. Uriah and other innocent casualties died that day, all because of the king's illicit tryst with Bathsheba and the baby they made together.

"Now when the wife of Uriah heard that Uriah her husband was dead, she mourned for her husband" (2 Samuel 11:26). We are not told how long newly pregnant Bathsheba sorrowed over her husband's sudden and untimely passing. One writer noted, "The official mourning period for an individual might have varied in duration, depending on the social status of the deceased: Aaron and Moses were officially mourned for one cycle of the moon (cf. Numbers 20:29 and Deuteronomy 34:8); Uriah's mourning period would not have exceeded that."[87] A lunar cycle is twenty-nine and a half days long.

"When the time of mourning was over, David sent and brought her to his house and she became his wife; then she bore him a son" (2 Samuel 11:27a). Just days after the shock of Uriah's death, Bathsheba found herself married to King David, living in his palace harem, and expecting his child. As women, we know that jumbled emotions can wreak havoc in our souls. Bathsheba would have been no different. I remember the gamut of emotions that overwhelmed me at times as my pregnancy hormones abounded. I can't begin to imagine all Bathsheba dealt with, considering the tremendous upheaval she faced in such a short time. To tie up loose ends and perhaps appear heroic in the aftermath of Uriah's death, David's solicitous actions toward Bathsheba may have squelched the rumor mill, but nothing can be hidden from God.

"But the thing that David had done was evil in the sight of the Lord" (2 Samuel 11:27b). This is the first mention of God in this sad chapter. Maybe the king thought he had done a pretty good job of covering up his sin. But God looks within and sees everything in our hearts. Not a single action, not even a single thought, can be hidden from Him. God always acts in perfect accordance with His sovereign will in every situation, even one as tragic as Bathsheba's.

"In this instance, 'the Lord sent Nathan to David,' apparently on the day that Bathsheba gave birth to the baby."[88] Two deliveries took place that fateful day: Bathsheba delivered their baby and Nathan delivered a message from God, who sent His prophet Nathan to paint a powerful word picture for David in 2 Samuel 12. It's such a genius approach! "There were two men in one city, the one rich and the other poor. The rich man had a great many flocks and herds. But the poor man had nothing except one little ewe lamb which he bought and nourished; and it grew up together with him and his children. It would eat of his bread and drink of his cup and lie in his bosom, and was like a daughter to him. Now a traveler came to the rich man, and he was unwilling to take from his own flock or his own herd, to prepare for the wayfarer who had come to him; rather he took the poor man's ewe lamb and prepared it for the man who had come to him" (2 Samuel 12:1–4).

Upon hearing this story, David's fury exploded. "As the Lord lives, surely the man who has done this deserves to die. He must make restitution for the lamb fourfold, because he did this thing and had no compassion.' Nathan then said to David, 'You are the man!'" (2 Samuel 12:5–7). Can you imagine that moment? His secret sin, exposed in all its ugliness, left him without any excuses. Nathan continued: "Thus says the Lord God of Israel, 'It is I who anointed you king over Israel and it is I who delivered you from the hand of Saul. I also gave you your master's house and your master's wives into your care, and I gave you the house of Israel and Judah; and if that had been too little, I would have added to you many more things like these! Why have you despised the word of the Lord by doing evil in His sight? You have struck down Uriah the Hittite with the sword, have taken his wife to be your wife, and have killed him with the sword of the sons of Ammon. Now therefore, the sword shall never depart from your house, because you have despised Me and have taken the wife of Uriah the Hittite to be your wife.' Thus says the Lord, 'Behold, I will raise up evil against you from your own household; I will even take your wives before your eyes and give them to your companion, and he will lie with your wives in broad daylight. Indeed you did it secretly, but I will do this thing before all Israel, and under the sun'" (2 Samuel 11:7–12).

You may remember the fulfillment of God's promised discipline when David's own son, Absalom, rebelled against David by defiantly engaging in sex with ten of David's concubines on a rooftop in plain view. Interestingly, it was Ahithophel, Bathsheba's grandfather, who advised Absalom to do this, perhaps on the very rooftop where David had seen and lusted after his granddaughter (2 Samuel 15:16, 16:21–23). We may wonder if Ahithophel had justice for his beautiful granddaughter in mind when he urged Absalom's rebellion.

Throughout his life, David had been the privileged recipient of God's lavished blessings, yet David "despised" God by resorting to his own selfish desires to bless himself. God told David that his evil actions translated into contempt for Him and His word. Whenever we turn our back on God's blessing and try to bless ourselves by yielding to sinful desires, we greatly displease God and we set into motion our deserved discipline from His righteous hand. Hebrews 12:6 is a timely reminder that, "For those whom the Lord loves He disciplines." Because God loved David, He laid out a plan of discipline for him.

"Then David said to Nathan, 'I have sinned against the Lord'" (2 Samuel 12:13). All sin is a violation of God's Word and whenever we sin it is God we offend the most. David recognized this. But Nathan then reassured David, "The Lord also has taken away your sin; you shall not die. However, because by this deed you have given occasion to the enemies of the Lord to blaspheme, the child also that is born to you shall surely die" (2 Samuel 11:13–14).

What a great reminder that the world is always watching us! Whenever believers, especially ones in the public arena, willingly fall into the cesspool of sin, the ripple effect gives rise to criticism, hurts everyone, and tarnishes the Lord's reputation. When David's sin with Bathsheba went public, it was like giving out free weapons to all his enemies with which to defeat him in battle. David's disregard for God's laws, as evidenced in his adultery with Bathsheba, also caused others to think less of his God as well.

Even forgiven sin can leave behind a residue of consequences. By choosing a specific course of action, David set into motion a series of consequences that had to be played out. Even though David repented and received God's forgiveness, Bathsheba couldn't become "un-pregnant." Uriah couldn't become "un-dead." A friend of mine once reminded me that we can choose our actions or we can choose our consequences, but we can't choose both at the same time. In other words, once we've decided upon a certain action, we need to be willing to live with the possible consequences of that action. And if we want a specific consequence to be true in our lives, our actions are predetermined to generate the desired outcome.

After Nathan returned to his home, "the Lord struck the child that Uriah's widow bore to David, so that he was very sick. David therefore inquired of God for the child; and David fasted and went and lay all night on the ground. The elders of his household stood beside him in order to raise him up from the ground, but he was unwilling and would not eat food with them. Then it happened on the seventh day that the child died. And the servants of David were afraid to tell him that the child was dead, for they said, 'Behold, while the child was still alive, we spoke to him and he did not listen to our voice. How then can we tell him that the child is dead, since he might do himself harm!' But when David saw that his servants were whispering together, David perceived that the child was dead; so David said to his servants, 'Is the child dead?' And they said, 'He is dead.' So David arose from the ground, washed, anointed himself, and changed his clothes; and he came into the house of the Lord and worshiped. Then he came to his own house, and when he requested, they set food before him and he ate. Then his servants said to him, 'What is this thing that you have done? While the child was alive, you fasted and wept; but when the child died, you arose and ate food.' He said, 'While the child was still alive, I fasted and wept; for I said, "Who knows, the Lord may be gracious to me, that the child may live." But now he has died; why should I fast? Can I bring him back again? I will go to him, but he will not return to me'" (2 Samuel 11:15–23).

Bathsheba's heart must have broken with the death of her precious week-old newborn. I've not experienced the loss of a child, but friends of mine have. One of my friends lost a baby boy years ago, but confessed that at times the grief still felt so fresh. Women who have given up babies for adoption also feel a similar grief as their loss can leave a gaping hole in their hearts. I picture a sobbing Bathsheba comforted by David as he perhaps held her close and cried with her.

I know women who have had babies out of wedlock or even from illicit relationships. This does **not** mean that God loves that child less than one from a relationship that honors Him. The fact that God took David and Bathsheba's first child to heaven to be with Him was part of David's discipline. The Lord disciplines all of us in ways that are for our own good and for His glory. The fact that David said he would see his baby again gives us great hope. Those for whom heaven is their eternal destination will one day be reunited with their babies who have died.

"Then David comforted his wife, Bathsheba, and went in to her and lay with her; and she gave birth to a son, and he named him Solomon. Now the Lord loved him" (2 Samuel 12:24). Their first sexual encounter took place secretly, perhaps quickly, forcefully, and guiltily. However, in this verse where David is recorded as again sleeping with Bathsheba, it is in the context of comforting her. I imagine their union this time as being sweet and tender. In addition, David had been assured through Nathan the prophet that the Lord had forgiven him. This time around, he would have been free from guilt, able to enjoy being with Bathsheba and having four additional sons with her (1 Chronicles 3:5). I love this confirmation of the Lord's forgiveness! Their relationship started out shrouded in sin and secrecy. Yet David acknowledged his sin and repented. As a result, David and Bathsheba's union enjoyed God's blessing in the form of more children. Their son, Solomon, grew up to become the next king of Israel, as well as the recipient of God's gifts of wisdom and riches.

Our next glimpse into Bathsheba's life takes place as David, now a very old man, lay dying. He had trouble keeping warm so a kingdom-wide search was conducted for the most beautiful virgin in the land. A girl by the name of Abishag won the beauty contest. She became David's private nurse and spent a lot of her time in bed with him to keep him warm. "The girl was very beautiful; and she became the king's nurse and served him, but the king did not cohabit with her" (1 Kings 1:1–4).

Meanwhile, Adonijah, one of David's sons, made a play for the throne and gathered enough support from those outside David's power circle to temporarily pull it off (1 Kings 1:5–10). So, Nathan the prophet approached Bathsheba to ask for her help in informing the king of this revolting development. Nathan cautioned her, "If you want to save your own life and the life of your son Solomon, follow my advice" (1 Kings 1:12, NLT). Bathsheba, perhaps still a beautiful woman, entered the king's bedchamber where Abishag ministered to him. She informed David of Adonijah's treasonous act and reminded him that he had promised her long ago that their son, Solomon, would become the next king. As she finished her speech, Nathan entered the room to verify Bathsheba's message (1 Kings 1:15–27).

Years earlier, King David had declared to the entire assembly of Israel, "My son Solomon, whom God has clearly chosen as the next king of Israel, is still young and inexperienced. The work ahead of him is enormous, for the Temple he will build is not for mere mortals—it is for the Lord God himself!" (1 Chronicles 29:1, NLT). Bathsheba, as one of the assembled people, would have heard David's message and known for some time that she would one day see her son seated on David's throne, in charge of building the temple.

The aged king wasted no time in addressing this tense situation. He called Bathsheba back into his room and as she stood before him, he told her, "I vowed to you by the Lord the God of Israel, saying, 'Your son Solomon shall be king after me, and he shall sit on my throne in my place'; I will indeed do so this day'" (1 Kings 1:30). Solomon officially became king, duly recognized by all the authorities in Israel. He graciously let his brother Adonijah live (1 Kings 1:28–53).

Unfortunately, Adonijah must have been very hardheaded and highly ambitious because he wasn't done with the power plays. He was also one spoiled boy! We find out why in 1 Kings 1. "Now his father, King David, had never disciplined him at any time, even by asking, 'Why are you doing that?'" (1 Kings 1:6, NLT). One day, Adonijah approached Bathsheba and begged her to ask King Solomon if he could marry Abishag. Perhaps he thought going through her would make his request less threatening. Or maybe he assumed Bathsheba had a measure of control over her son Solomon. Or, perhaps Bathsheba knew how Solomon would react and she wanted his decisive action regarding Adonijah broadcast to the nation to help the Israelites feel more secure under a wise and unifying king. Whatever her rationale, Bathsheba agreed.

As Bathsheba entered the throne room, King Solomon had his officials place a throne on his right so his mother could sit in a place of honor beside him. When Bathsheba voiced Adonijah's request, Solomon saw it for what it was, another attempt at his throne. Even though David never had sex with Abishag, she was still considered one of his wives and part of David's regime, which now belonged to Solomon. One author observed, "Bathsheba, who in some parts of her story appears a 'helpless female' (1 Kings 1:11–16), in fact wields great power. She intervenes for Solomon with David, and attempts to intervene when Solomon's banished brother Adonijah asks for her to help him obtain Abishag, David's concubine. Solomon seemingly responds scathingly to Bathsheba's public request in Adonijah's name, however, Bathsheba may have been setting the scene for Solomon to make a show of public strength. Song of Solomon 3:11 reveals the significance of Bathsheba's role: 'King Solomon wearing the crown, the crown with which his mother crowned him on the day of his wedding.'"[89]

The king had Adonijah put to death that very day. And this is the last glimpse we have of Bathsheba, honored by her son the king, and sitting on a throne at his right hand (1 Kings 2:13–24). In the beginning of her story, we see her entering the palace, under cover of darkness, the king unwilling for any to see her, or know what he was doing to her. In the end, she is sitting on a throne in the palace, in full view of all, enjoying high privileges as Queen Mother. Bathsheba lived long enough to witness how the Lord "exalted Solomon in the sight of all Israel, and he gave Solomon greater royal splendor than any king in Israel before him (1 Chronicles 29:25, NLT).

As a gifted writer and composer, David exposed his life with honest transparency and fragile vulnerability. He never shied away from sharing deep emotions and heart-wrenching sorrows in so many of his psalms. So, it should come as no surprise that he chronicled his affair with Bathsheba and his desire for forgiveness in Psalm 51. The heading for this psalm reads, "For the choir director." Because so many servants, guards, and messengers knew about David's involvement with Bathsheba, David realized his sin had gone public. In writing these words set to music, David knew his song would spread throughout the land. This was a huge deal on his part. He truly humbled himself before his entire nation. I wouldn't want to turn my sins into a song that others would know and sing, but I'm grateful that David, under the guidance of the Holy Spirit, did just that!

The heading continues, "A Psalm of David, when Nathan the prophet came to him, after he had gone in to Bathsheba." After that pride-crushing encounter with Nathan, perhaps David sought a place of solitude where he could have a private and uninterrupted conversation with God. As he poured out his heart, this prayer, bathed in bitter tears, became a beautiful song of confession and forgiveness.

Be gracious to me, O God, according to Your lovingkindness; according to the greatness of Your compassion blot out my transgressions. Wash me thoroughly from my iniquity and cleanse me from my sin. For I know my transgressions, and my sin is ever before me. Against You, You only, I have sinned and done what is evil in Your sight, so that You are justified when You speak and blameless when You judge. Behold, I was brought forth in iniquity, and in sin my mother conceived me. Behold, You desire truth in the innermost being, and in the hidden part You will make me know wisdom. Purify me with hyssop, and I shall be clean; wash me, and I shall be whiter than snow. Make me to hear joy and gladness, let the bones which You have broken rejoice. Hide Your face from my sins and blot out all my iniquities. Create in me a clean heart, O God, and renew a steadfast spirit within me. Do not cast me away from Your presence and do not take Your Holy Spirit from me. Restore to me the joy of Your salvation and sustain me with a willing spirit. Then I will teach transgressors Your ways, and sinners will be converted to You. Deliver me from bloodguiltiness, O God, the God of my salvation; then my tongue will joyfully sing of Your righteousness. O Lord, open my lips, that my mouth may declare Your praise" (Psalm 51:1–15).

Birthed from tragedy and heartbreaking pain, this beautiful Psalm teaches us seven truths about confession and seven truths about forgiveness. These eternal principles were true for David and Bathsheba then, and are just as true for us today.

Seven Truths About Confession from Psalm 51:1-15

Confession recognizes my rebellion.

David looked within and could say, "For I know my transgressions" (Psalm 51:3). He knew his rebellion began the moment he acted upon his lust for Bathsheba. As one who loved to meditate on God's commands, he would have been familiar with the portion of Exodus 20:17 which commands, "You shall not covet your neighbor's wife." His rebellion escalated when he disregarded God's Word and decided to live outside God's laws by committing adultery with Bathsheba and then murdering her husband. With a humble heart, David wrote, "I will confess my rebellious acts to the Lord" (Psalm 32:5, NET).

Unconfessed sin will haunt me day and night.

After many troubled days and restless nights, David had to say, "My sin is ever before me" (Psalm 51:3). His secret and sinful liaison with Bathsheba translated into miserable days and sleepless nights. The nights he was trying to get Uriah to go home to Bathsheba would have been restless ones as he tossed and turned, planning the next step if that one failed. And it only got worse. When the baby was born and immediately became quite sick, David stopped eating and lay on the ground for seven nights in a row. He became a haunted man indeed. David admitted to God, "For day and night Your hand was heavy upon me" (Psalm 32:4).

Confession acknowledges my sin has offended God.

David got to the heart of the matter when he confessed, "Against You, You only, I have sinned" (Psalm 51:4). David's sin hurt Bathsheba, damaged his close friendships with her grandfather and father, killed her husband Uriah and other soldiers, resulted in the death of his newborn son, and disappointed so many of his followers. But most of all, he offended his holy God.

Confession realizes my sin is evil in God's sight.

Sin is sin, even a little "white lie" is sin, and all of it is evil in God's sight. We can't whitewash it, try to hide it, wish it away, rationalize it, excuse it, or even trivialize it. It took God sending Nathan to David to paint a picture of the magnitude of his sin. As one who lived to study God's law and write songs about it, David clearly knew what a holy God thought about sin. With everything exposed in the light of day, David had to tell the truth and admit he had done what was evil in God's sight (Psalm 51:4).

Confession helps me be honest about my sins.

David named his sins and held nothing back; even admitting he had shed blood when he arranged Uriah's death. David asked God to deliver him "from bloodguiltiness, O God, the God of my salvation" (Psalm 51:14). It is painful, yet cathartic, to honestly face our sins, refusing to keep them hidden, and instead, bring them out into the light of day. David knew what God desired. "Behold, You desire truth in the innermost being" (Psalm 51:6).

Confession declares God's right to judge me.

God is holy. He is the perfectly righteous Judge. David told God in his prayer, "You are justified when You speak and blameless when You judge" (Psalm 51:4). God cannot lie. He will never deny His Word. His words and character will always prove His righteousness and His right to judge. David also admitted, even after the heartache of losing a child, that God's judgment of him was right, fair, and just.

Confession asks for help in the future.

David lamented, "Behold, I was brought forth in iniquity, and in sin my mother conceived me" (Psalm 51:5). Anyone who has ever had a baby or been around small children knows that human beings are born with a sin nature. When our granddaughter Fiona, two at the time, asked if she could watch the baby channel on the TV in our bedroom, I said she had to get permission from her Daddy first. Josh was in another part of the house, but I happened to hear him tell her "No, honey, not right now." Fiona raced back to me as fast as her little legs could carry her and exclaimed, "Maybe Daddy said 'yes!'" Even the most adorable little girls on earth come equipped with a fallen sin nature!

David begged God, "Restore to me the joy of Your salvation and sustain me with a willing spirit" (Psalm 51:12). I like how this verse reads in another translation, "Make me willing to obey you" (NLT). David realized that obedience is an act of the will that begins in the mind and that's where he needed God's help.

Seven Truths About God's Forgiveness from Psalm 51:1-15

God's forgiveness is ours for the asking.

David must have felt so dirty carrying around his unconfessed sin. We see the following phrases from Psalm 51 that characterize cleansing:

"Blot out my transgressions" (verse 1).
"Wash me thoroughly from my iniquity" (verse 2).
"Cleanse me from my sin" (verse 2).
"Purify me with hyssop and I shall be clean" (verse 7).
"Wash me, and I shall be whiter than snow" (verse 7).
"Blot out all my iniquities" (verse 9).
"Create in me a clean heart" (verse 10).

David asked all this of God because he knew only God's forgiveness could wash away all his sins.

God's forgiveness flows out of His mercy, unfailing love, and great compassion for us.

David begged God to have mercy on him because he knew God is full of compassion and unfailing love. The truth that God loves us unconditionally and continually makes little difference in our lives if we refuse to believe it and act upon it. A picture I use helps me appropriate this truth. I imagine that poised above my head is a large watering can, tilted to pour out on me continually, following me wherever I go. But instead of water, it's God's love that is continually pouring out, drenching me, and overflowing all around me. This watering can will never run dry. And absolutely nothing can separate me from it. When any unpleasant, stressful, or painful situation is happening in my life, I try to stop whatever I'm doing or feeling, and know that at that very instant, I am being covered and saturated with God's overflowing, never-ending, unconditional love for me.

God's forgiveness blots out the stains of our sins.

David pleaded with God, "Don't keep looking at my sins. Remove the stain of my guilt" (Psalm 51:9, NLT). Have you ever been out in public and suddenly noticed a highly visible stain on your clothing? You become acutely aware of that stain, you wonder how many other people have seen it, and can you keep your arms crossed to hide it? We know nothing but stain remover can help. Convicted and contrite, David sees his stained heart and knows only God can eradicate this stain for good.

God's forgiveness washes us clean from our guilt and purifies us.

David asked God to, "Purify me with hyssop, and I shall be clean" (Psalm 51:7). The first mention of hyssop in Scripture occurs within the context of Passover in Exodus 12. This first Passover took place in Egypt while the Israelites were still in bondage. They were to take an unblemished year-old male lamb, sacrifice it, and collect some of its blood. Then, using a sprig of hyssop, they were to dip it in the blood and paint some on the doorposts and lintels of their houses. As they stayed in their homes behind doorways marked with blood, shed in sacrifice for sin, a sign of their obedience to God and trust in His word, God passed over them to execute His righteous judgment against all who worshipped the false gods of Egypt. Those whose homes were not protected by the shed blood experienced great sorrow as their firstborn passed away suddenly in the night. David used the metaphor of hyssop, asking God to cleanse him based on the blood of the substitutionary sacrifice. David recognized that according to Leviticus 17:11, "The life of the flesh is in the blood, and I have given it to you on the altar to make atonement for your souls; for it is the blood by reason of the life that makes atonement." As believers, we marvel at all the connections between Passover and the sacrifice of Jesus who shed His blood on the cross for our sins. When by faith we believe in Him, we are washed clean and saved from everlasting punishment.

God's forgiveness restores our joy.

I like to define joy as a contented resting in God, a deep-seated satisfaction in Him. David lost his joy the moment he began living in sin. His actions were at war with God's commands. After spending almost a year at odds with his God, when he repented and received full forgiveness, his joy must have felt explosive! He could write, "How blessed is he whose transgression is forgiven, whose sin is covered!" (Psalm 32:1). Another translation reads, "Oh, what joy for those whose disobedience is forgiven, whose sin is put out of sight!" (NLT).

God's forgiveness rinses our hearts clean and renews our relationship with Him.

Carrying around a burden of unconfessed sin would have made David feel so dirty and heavy in spirit. He begged, "Create in me a clean heart, O God, and renew a steadfast spirit within me. Do not cast me away from Your presence and do not take Your Holy Spirit from me" (Psalm 51:10–11). In Ephesians 4:30, Paul cautions "Do not grieve the Holy Spirit of God, by whom you were sealed for the day of redemption." Just as disobedient children grieve our hearts, God's heart is grieved when His children are out of fellowship with Him by living in disobedience.

One of my all-time favorite verses is 1 John 1:9, "If we confess our sins, He is faithful and righteous to forgive us our sins and to cleanse us from all unrighteousness." God's forgiveness has the power to cleanse me from **all** unrighteousness. Sometimes people assume that their sin is so serious that it is unforgivable. However, that line of reasoning makes the false assumption that God is not all-powerful, and that our sin is stronger than His forgiveness. No sin is too great that it can't be forgiven. How encouraging!

God's forgiveness makes us want to be more obedient in the future.

David recognized that a walk of obedience required God's super-natural help. He prayed, "Sustain me with a willing [obedient] spirit"

(Psalm 51:12). When we fall into sin, we grieve God and damage our fellowship with Him. The healing process of confessing our sins and receiving His forgiveness should serve to reinforce our desire to obey Him better in the future as we receive His cleansing and luxuriate in His lavish grace. Confession is simply agreeing with God that what we have done is wrong.

David's prolific songwriting may have suffered during his months of estrangement from God, but once he confessed his sins and received God's forgiveness, it's not hard to imagine that his words of praise to God flowed freely again. David wrote, "O Lord, open my lips, that my mouth may declare Your praise" (Psalm 51:15). When David received God's bountiful forgiveness, he could exclaim, "My tongue will joyfully sing of Your righteousness" (Psalm 51:14).

As one entangled in David's sin, Bathsheba closely witnessed David's spiritual struggle that gave birth to this psalm. As his wife, she heard his words and probably learned the melody so that she, too, could sing this song. In fact, after experiencing God's restoring forgiveness, David had a new mission! He promised, "Then I will teach transgressors Your ways, and sinners will be converted to You" (Psalm 51:13). Linked to him through marriage, perhaps Bathsheba became one of those sinners converted to God! Despite their tragic beginning, Bathsheba's remaining years with David received divine blessing because the king lived out the rest of his days striving to please his God. "For David had done what was pleasing in the Lord's sight and had obeyed the Lord's commands throughout his life, except in the affair concerning Uriah the Hittite" (1 Kings 5:5, NLT).

My longtime friend, Heather (fictitious name), appeared to be at death's door. She could barely walk, she had to quit her part-time job, she had zero energy—even her hair looked dull and had stopped growing. Seeing her this way frightened me. Her husband told us he despaired of her ever getting better. Heather called one day to invite us to dinner and her voice sounded different and upbeat. As we greeted each other, I could hardly believe my eyes. She positively glowed. She had energy. She was back to working fulltime and even taking dance lessons. She looked years younger. The transformation was startling. During dinner, she recounted her story.

As a last-ditch effort, Heather had decided to try one more doctor to help her. This doctor happened to be a believer who specialized in holistic medicine. As he examined her, he inquired carefully about her life story. Heather had been the unfortunate victim of incest. Her father had repeatedly sexually molested her for a number of years. She had never been able to forgive him. The doctor wondered whether her physical issues had anything to do with the deep anger she harbored toward her father. Heather, a longtime believer, knew the doctor had uncovered the root of her problem. With God's help, she fully and freely forgave her deceased father for all the harm he had inflicted. With the poison of unforgiveness released from her body, she quickly recovered full health. Author Corrie Ten Boom said this about survivors of the Holocaust, "Those who were able to forgive their former enemies were able also to return to the outside world and rebuild their lives, no matter what the physical scars. Those who nursed their bitterness remained invalids. It was as simple and as horrible as that."[90]

As believers, it's important to forgive ourselves when God forgives us. We don't have to hold on to guilt and shame. You may ask, but what about all the times we keep remembering the forgiven offenses, the ones we've committed or ones that have been committed against us? Our human minds store memories; that's what God made them to do. We need to engage in an exercise of reminder and renewal. Whenever the offense pops up, we should immediately remind ourselves that God has forgiven it, and then ask Him to renew our minds with His truth.

One author insightfully defined the difference between forgetting and forgiving when he wrote, "Forgetting is a biological function and forgiving is a spiritual function." In one of his books he explained that the key is to have the spiritual function of forgiving render powerless the biological function of remembering.[91] Remembering offenses can dredge up painful emotions and bitter memories, reminding us that we need to forgive again. Proverbs 17:9 speaks directly to this when it states, "Love prospers when a fault is forgiven, but dwelling on it separates close friends." (NLT) My husband once experienced a betrayal that cost friendships and financial hardship. He told me that every time he thought about it, or dealt with the damage this person caused, he had to choose to forgive all over again.

It's also important to remember that by extending forgiveness we are not excusing the offense or pretending it never happened. It did. Rather, each time we extend forgiveness, we are consciously relinquishing our right to punish the offender. Romans 12:19 is very clear. "Never take your own revenge, beloved, but leave room for the wrath of God, for it is written, 'Vengeance is mine, I will repay' says the Lord." Let God keep the record in His books of everything done against you. Let God administer the punishment for you. That way you'll be free, and according to 1 Corinthians 13:5, you won't have to keep any kind of record of being wronged. Please don't waste one more minute of your life harboring poisonous unforgiveness. It's such an angry and bitter prison of your own making. I encourage you to discover divine release from the chains of unforgiveness and revel in the freedom that God's gracious forgiveness provides.

At this point, it might be helpful to ask some questions that will help surface any need for forgiveness in your own life: Are you harboring any unforgiveness? Is there someone to whom you need to extend forgiveness? Do you need to ask God to forgive you for anything?

I recall a time when the Lord clearly showed me I was living in a prison of unforgiveness. One of my extended relatives offended me during my teenage years. Circumstances dictated that our paths crossed daily for a time. As the recipient of an often judgmental and critical spirit, I felt defeated, inferior, and sometimes unwanted. Realizing that I carried baggage from our past relationship into my present, I asked God to help me be free from the ongoing negative internal dialogue influencing my thoughts. My relative was deceased by the time I was ready to deal with this, so I went upstairs to a bonus room in our house, placed two chairs facing each other in the middle of the room, and imaginatively sat this relative on one, while I occupied the other. Out loud, I rehearsed all the ways and times I had been hurt, dredging up each painful memory. Then I said, "But I fully forgive you, _____, because Jesus has fully forgiven me. I realize that I have offended Him far more than you ever offended me. I release the burden of unforgiveness I have been carrying around. Today, and from now on, I refuse to grant power or give credence to my hurt-filled memories. I am walking out of my prison. It's over. It's all forgiven and I am free!"

Father God, thank You for including sordid stories of sin in Your holy Word because we can all relate to the devastation sin has caused in our own lives. How thankful we are that forgiveness is ours for the asking! Whenever we are tempted to remember what has already been forgiven, I pray You would help us to quickly replace that debilitating thought with this reminder from Isaiah 43:25, "I, even I, am the One who wipes out your transgressions for My own sake, and I will not remember your sins."

If you choose to not remember the sins You have forgiven, I pray You would help us do the same. How we praise You for Your faithful promise to forgive our sins when we confess them to You. How we praise You for washing our sin-stained hearts by cleansing us from all unrighteousness. We pray You would enable us to choose obedient actions that result in righteous consequences so that we may enjoy an unhindered love-walk with You. Amen.

Focus Points

1. What triggers the sin process according to James 1:14–15? What happens when sin becomes full-grown?

2. How could David have prevented his sin with Bathsheba?

3. In Nehemiah chapter 9, the Israelites are recorded publically confessing their sins to God. In verse 3, what activity did they engage in before confession?
    Why do you think that was important?
    What accompanied their confession?
    According to verse 17, which divine attributes always accompany God's forgiveness?

4. In Psalm 103:12, we are assured that God's forgiveness is lasting. How far has He removed our forgiven sins from us? Can that be measured?

5. Using Matthew 5:23–24 as our guide, if we know another believer has something against us, what does Jesus tell us to do about it? Have you ever put this passage into practice? If so, describe what happened.

6. How often are we to forgive others who offend or hurt us according to Matthew 18:21–22?

7. It's human nature to remember offenses and hold grudges. If we want to embody the love of Christ to others, 1 Corinthians 13:5 encourages us refrain from which actions?

8. For which reasons should we give joyful thanks to God according to Colossians 1:12–14?

9. Is there any unconfessed sin in your life? Ask God to reveal it to you. He will! If there is, confess it and ask for forgiveness. Then believe He has granted it to you fully and freely.

10. Is there anyone who has hurt or wronged you that you need to forgive? Remember that you can forgive someone even if they never seek it from you. Forgive them just as God has forgiven you and you'll be set free!

V

Ezekiel's Wife: Being Strong

When someone remarks, "She's a strong woman," we may think: controlling, energetic, stubborn, highly opinionated, athletic, or even stoic. When someone comments, "She's a godly woman," we may think: close walk with God, selfless, involved in serving the church, reads the Bible, prays a lot, leads people to Christ and disciples them. When we read about the Proverbs 31 Woman in Scripture, we may think: unrealistic, impossible standards, unattainable goals, and intimidating to the max. In this chapter, we will examine all three motifs as we meet a very obscure woman from perhaps an unused portion of our Bible, the book of Ezekiel. My husband calls this lesser read section of Scripture, "the white pages!"

Until I began reading through the Bible on a yearly basis, I had no idea Ezekiel even had a wife! I remember being shocked the first time I read about her sudden death. Her brief, but important story in Ezekiel 24:15–24 intrigued me. I began to wonder what her life must have been like. As I imagined her going through some of the difficulties that accompanied marriage to the unusual prophet, Ezekiel, I kept getting the impression of a very strong woman.

Along with Ezekiel's wife, we will also be looking at the Proverbs 31 Woman. As we combine their stories, a realistic picture will emerge of the characteristics of a strong and godly woman that will encourage us with practical ways in which we can become more like them. Let's meet Ezekiel's wife first.

To be clear, we have no idea when Ezekiel married. However, if their lives followed the normal pattern of the day, an arranged marriage would have taken place when they were young, perhaps in their late teens or early twenties. We are not given the name of Ezekiel's wife in his book so I'm going to refer to her as *Ishshah*,[92] the Hebrew word for woman and wife. Ezekiel, whose name means *God will strengthen*,[93] was born in the land of Judah. Perhaps he met his wife there, or maybe he met her in Babylon among the exiles.

When we are first introduced to Ezekiel, it's with the title, "Ezekiel the priest." Cognizant of his priestly lineage, Ishshah would have been familiar with the fact that Ezekiel could expect to join the priesthood at age thirty (Numbers 4:3).[94] Perhaps she assumed their lives would revolve around his priestly duties and activities. She may have observed other priests' wives and noticed how they fulfilled their roles and coped with demanding lives. Despite growing apostasy in the land of Judah, there were still some priests who remained faithful to God, Ezekiel being one of them.

During Ezekiel's day, we may wonder what his fellow Israelites thought about their situation. "In spite of the conquest of Judah by the Babylonians in 605 BC, the Hebrew people were convinced of two things. First, they believed Jerusalem was inviolable. Though they had suffered the temporary setback of Babylonian domination, their city was still under Jewish administration. The city was the seat of Yahweh worship (Psalm 48:1–14), and thus the people believed it would never be destroyed or fall to a pagan power. Second, they believed that those taken captive in 605 BC would be in Babylon only a short time. They were sure that friends, relatives, and leaders taken hostage to Babylon would be coming home soon."[95] The prophet Daniel was among those taken captive and transported to Babylon in 605 BC. Ezekiel, born in 622 BC, would have been seventeen years old.

Though loved ones lived under captivity in Babylon, and turbulent times assaulted their homeland in the form of foreign domination and enemy oppression, life went on. Young people married, had babies, and established homes. However, as part of God's judgment on a nation embroiled in rebellion, He allowed King Nebuchadnezzar from Babylon to attack Jerusalem and gain control of the city in 597 BC (2 Kings 24:10–12). Ezekiel, age twenty-five, and his wife, presumably the same age or younger, were included in this second wave of people taken captive to Babylon.

What must that have felt like—to be captured and carried away to a foreign land against their will? When my parents sensed God calling them to move our family from Portland, Oregon to San Jose, Costa Rica, they didn't consult my siblings or me, the oldest of their five children. Because we were so young, ranging in age from one to eight, they simply informed us we were moving. Leaving behind the familiar comforts of home, my best friend, and grandparents living in the States, was very difficult. I had just finished the third grade and suddenly we were living in Costa Rica so my parents could learn Spanish at language school in preparation for ministry in Argentina. I found myself struggling through fourth grade, desperately trying to understand anything in my all-Spanish school. The teacher took pity on my sad situation and each day plopped a new stack of magazines on my desk to flip through while the other students engaged in learning. Thankfully, my parents eventually moved me to another school that taught in English so fourth grade could be somewhat salvaged. I know a little of what it's like to be thrust onto the fast track of tremendous change and upheaval.

Ezekiel and Ishshah had to make hard and constant adjustments to their new surroundings as well. One of the psalms graphically describes this heartbreaking time of captivity in Babylon. "By the rivers of Babylon there we sat down and wept when we remembered Zion. Upon the willows in the midst of it we hung our harps. For there our captors demanded of us songs, and our tormentor's mirth, saying 'Sing us one of the songs of Zion.' How can we sing the Lord's song in a foreign land?'" (Psalm 137:1–4). The last thing the captives felt like doing was singing the songs of Zion, of home, as hanging their harps on tree limbs by the river so poignantly portrayed. Their captors took perverse delight in taunting them; demanding they perform songs from their homeland, but the music had died in their hearts.

They may have questioned God's plan for them in this foreign and hostile land, but God's word to the prophet Jeremiah revealed His sovereign design for Ishshah and her husband. God showed Jeremiah a vision of two baskets of figs placed in front of the temple in Jerusalem, one full of good figs, the other, filled with bad figs. Then the Lord told Jeremiah "The good figs represent the exiles I sent from Judah to the land of the Babylonians. I will watch over and care for them, and I will bring them back here again. I will build them up and not tear them down. I will plant them and not uproot them. I will give them hearts that recognize me as the Lord. They will be my people, and I will be their God, for they will return to me wholeheartedly" (Jeremiah 24:4–7). As "good figs," Ezekiel and Ishshah could be assured of God's loving watchcare over them, even when living under duress in a strange land.

The prophet Jeremiah also sent the captives this encouraging word from God, designed to bolster their spirits and provide instructions for life in Babylon. "Thus says the Lord of hosts, the God of

Israel, to all the exiles whom I have sent into exile from Jerusalem to Babylon. Build houses and live in them; and plant gardens and eat their produce. Take wives and become the fathers of sons and daughters, and take wives for your sons and give your daughters to husbands, that they may bear sons and daughters; multiply there and do not decrease. Seek the welfare of the city where I have sent you into exile, and pray to the Lord on its behalf; for in its welfare you will have welfare . . . For I know the plans that I have for you, declares the Lord, plans for welfare and not for calamity to give you a future and a hope" (Jeremiah 29:4–11).

Ezekiel and Ishshah, along with the other captives, undoubtedly felt encouraged to know that God had orchestrated their exile into Babylon. Life would go on. They were to build houses, marry, have children, plant gardens, and even pray for Babylon's welfare so they could enjoy the benefits of their enemy's prosperity. The captives settled by the Kebar River, an offshoot of the Euphrates (Ezekiel 1:1). "The Kebar River was a man-made canal used for irrigation. This canal brought water from the Euphrates River for use in agricultural irrigation. Excavations at Babylon have revealed evidence of Jewish settlements along such a canal. Foreign countries were considered unclean habitations. The exiles probably would seek running water to use in ritual purification prior to prayer or other religious observances."[96]

Living in a foreign land, Ishshah may have struggled to make do while waiting for her garden to flourish. Like most wives, she worked hard to make the best home she could, even under trying circumstances. It helped to not be alone in this new place. Surrounded by so many friends in the same plight must have cheered her. According to 2 Kings 24:10–16, Ezekiel and Ishshah were part of a massive group of more than ten thousand fellow exiles: King Jehoiachin, his wives, his mother, his servants, his captains, and all the craftsmen and smiths. In fact, only the poorest of the people remained behind in Judah to farm the land.

Far from home, held captive under Babylon's rule, the couple found ways to cope with new realities. Had they remained in Jerusalem, Ezekiel would have been enjoying regular priestly duties centered on temple activities. Radical changes often require drastic mental adjustments as we seek to regain emotional equilibrium. When Mark proposed, I knew we would be married in Arizona, and then two months later move to Oregon to attend seminary. I knew he sought advanced Bible training to help him with the gospel presentation part of his magic shows. He planned to have a ministry as a traveling magician. Mark showed great talent in this area and I fully believed that would be our life—magic shows and travel. However, over the course of several years, I noticed a shift in Mark's interests. I watched him fall more deeply in love with God's Word and become gifted in preaching and teaching it. I had ample warning that our future life of traveling and magic shows might change to preaching in churches and teaching in a college or seminary setting.

Ishshah had no idea of the special plans God had for her husband. With no warning whatsoever, Ezekiel, on the fifth day of the fourth month of the year, July 31, 593 BC,[97] while living among the exiles by the Kebar River, saw and heard something so startling he was unable to communicate with anyone for seven days. In this mind-boggling vision, for his eyes only, the heavens opened, revealing stunning scenes (Ezekiel 1:1).

In his first spectacular vision from heaven, Ezekiel saw whirling wheels covered with eyes that moved multidirectionally. He saw four living beings unlike any he had ever seen. He saw fire and lightning and creatures beyond imagination. He saw figures flying with multiple pairs of wings. He saw the radiant glory of the Lord. This was a sound and light show of massive proportions! He heard the roar of rushing waters and the voice of God Himself. After seeing and hearing such overwhelming sights and sounds, Ezekiel fell flat on his face (Ezekiel 1:28).

At the end of this vision he was told to stand to his feet and receive his prophetic mandate. The Lord had clear instructions for this thirty-year-old: "Son of man, I have appointed you as a watchman for Israel. Whenever you receive a message from me, warn people immediately. If I warn the wicked, saying 'You are under the penalty of death,' but you fail to deliver the warning, they will die in their sins. And I will hold you responsible for their deaths" (Ezekiel 3:17–18, NLT). This divine appointment marked a turning point for Ezekiel. "Ezekiel the priest became Ezekiel the prophet of Yahweh."[98]

As God's mouthpiece to a rebellious people, Ezekiel's mission would not be easy. God informed him, "You shall speak My words to them whether they listen or not, for they are rebellious" (Ezekiel 2:7). What a tough assignment! Imagine if we were asked to deliver a series of messages to a group of people who showed no interest at all in what we were saying. We could easily become too discouraged to continue. I love how God promised to make Ezekiel as hard and obstinate about delivering God's messages to the people as they were in their determination not to listen (Ezekiel 3:8–9). Perhaps the meaning of his name, *God will strengthen*, served as a continual reminder to him that God would be his divine source of strength in this most difficult calling. After receiving his marching orders, Ezekiel was handed a scroll covered with writings full of sorrow and commanded to eat it. When Ezekiel ate the scroll, it tasted as sweet as honey in his mouth (Ezekiel 3:1–3). Isn't that exactly how God's Word should taste to us!

Psalm 19:10–11 describes God's words, even the ones that contain warnings, as sweeter than honey!

When Ezekiel awakened from the visions, he was still by the Kebar River among the exiles. Ezekiel 3:15 records that he sat there in a trance-like state for seven days, causing great consternation. What a tough week that must have been for Ishshah! Her young husband unable to tell her what was wrong with him. She may have feared for his sanity and health. I know of an associate pastor who battled deep depression from time to time. During one such episode, his young wife confided that he spent hours crying, unable to communicate coherently with her. As she parented their young children, she told me how much more she sympathized with single mothers, as her husband grew unable to help care for the children. For a time, his mother moved into their home to be a support to them. I marveled at this young woman's faith in God and her ability to remain strong for her husband. Certainly, Ishshah's strength ministered to her husband as he digested the magnitude of all that had been revealed to him.

At the end of those seven silent days, the Lord spoke once more, telling him to leave the river and go out to the plain where God would once again show him His glory and reveal more instructions for him to follow as recorded in Ezekiel 3:16–23. Upon returning to the settlement, he headed straight for his house. Under the Spirit's guidance he was instructed to "Go, shut yourself up in your house" (Ezekiel 3:24). And then Ezekiel received some very hard news, "Moreover, I will make your tongue stick to the roof of your mouth so that you will be mute" (Ezekiel 3:26). For the next seven and one-half years, his only audible speaking involved delivering God's messages to the people. Other than preaching God's words of judgment to the exiled people, Ezekiel remained mute.[99] That would be so hard, especially on his wife. Communication between them as a couple may have turned woefully one-sided!

"When Ezekiel's total ministry is examined, we see that he never ministered in the streets and assemblies of the people as other prophets did. The normal prophet moved among his people, reacting to the issues of his day right on the spot. Not Ezekiel. He ministered to the people through a strange immobility. The elders and the people came to him to inquire from the Lord."[100] We might imagine some of the challenges Ishshah faced as she juggled housework, meals, and perhaps child-rearing, all while entertaining numerous visitors to their home. Her front door symbolized the proverbial revolving door, granting precious little privacy in her own home. As word spread far and wide about this most unusual prophet acting out the strangest things, people would have been coming and going at all hours to behold this extreme visual aid from God. So where did she go for a much-needed break from the hectic pace of her life? Maybe a friend or relative invited her over for some conversation and a shared meal. Perhaps she enjoyed a special secluded spot by the Kebar River where she could spend a little time alone every now and then.

Ezekiel's ministry included some memorable visual aids to illustrate and expand upon his teaching. In the days of his confinement, he constructed a very elaborate display of objects and then used his own actions to reinforce the message. First, he took a brick and wrote the name Jerusalem on it; next he built a model battle site with tents and battering ramps. As he lay down on his side facing the brick and battle setting, he placed an iron plate between his face and the objects he had carefully arranged on the floor of his house. Even in this supine position, Ezekiel continued to deliver messages from God to the people. This elaborate exhibit served to warn the Israelites of impending judgment and hard times. Food and water would be rationed as Jerusalem was laid siege to by enemy forces. Some scholars believe Ezekiel only spent a portion of each day lying on his side, tethered to the floor, but even that created difficulties (Ezekiel 4:1–8).

Ishshah probably watched all this activity with her mouth wide open in surprised astonishment. Semi-mute, he could not verbally explain his bizarre actions to her. How long was Ezekiel to be tied to the floor of his home, and why? Ezekiel 4:4–6 explains: "Now lie on your left side and place the sins of Israel on yourself. You are to bear their sins for the number of days you lie there on your side. I am requiring you to bear Israel's sins for 390 days—one day for each year of their sin. After that, turn over and lie on your right side for 40 days—one day for each year of Judah's sin" (NLT).

Ishshah could not feed her husband any of her home-cooked meals during this prolonged time. Instead, Ezekiel's instructions from God demanded he mix six kinds of grains into a jar, pour out a set amount, stir in some liquid, shape it into a flat cake and then cook it over cow dung. He could only eat a rationed amount of food each day. His drinking water was also rationed. Why? As further discipline for the people's disobedience, God explained that Ezekiel's extreme visual aid reflected what would be happening in Jerusalem. "They will eat bread by weight and with anxiety, and drink water by measure and in horror, because bread and water will be scarce; and they will be appalled with one another and waste away in their iniquity" (Ezekiel 4:16–17). I wonder if Ezekiel's body wasted away as well, due to his restricted caloric intake.

Some grocery stores carry loaves of bread, often in the freezer section, labeled Ezekiel 4:9, using the same list of ingredients mentioned in this passage. Ishshah made sure her storage jars remained stocked with those six crucial grains: wheat, barley, beans, lentils, millet, and emmer wheat. I sometimes have a slice of this bread for breakfast.

It's delicious toasted, and spread with a little butter and honey. But if that's all I could eat every day for four hundred and thirty days, I would soon be sick of it. Imagine the torture of smelling meat and vegetables grilling over the fire and not be able to have any! Perhaps Ishshah took special pains to not cook or eat in front of him.

Ezekiel probably communicated his thoughts or needs to Ishshah in writing or sign language. Perhaps Ishshah experienced frustration because it required extra time and effort to communicate with her husband. I am very impressed with how this dear woman committed to staying by his side even though life with him remained far from normal! Perhaps she even had to position pots in close reach so that Ezekiel could relieve himself while lying on the floor. There may have been days when she longed for her homeland and the more predictable role of a priest's wife.

Her husband's appearance changed drastically one day when God commanded him to shave his head and beard with a barber's razor as yet another visual aid for the people of Jerusalem's coming desolation (Ezekiel 5:1–4). As a man who grew up expecting to become a priest, he knew all the regulations regarding biblical priesthood. One directive involved the priest's hair. "They shall not make any baldness on their heads, nor shave off the edges of their beards, nor make any cuts in their flesh" (Leviticus 21:5). This act would have further confirmed God's change of direction for Ezekiel, from that of a priest to a prophet. Perhaps Ishshah had never seen her husband hairless and it might have taken some getting used to! Did she cry, or laugh, or both, at the sight of her newly shorn husband? One rushed morning, before Mark left to teach a class, he asked me to trim his hair. He was in a hurry, which made me in a hurry, and the result was pretty hysterical, to me at least! His wavy hair is tricky to cut and by the time I finished clipping, some of his thick, dark hair stuck straight up and his forehead featured very short bangs. His college students tried unsuccessfully to hide their laughter at his new look. That was the first, and last time, I took scissors to his head!

During Ezekiel's ministry, the Lord showed him heartbreaking visions of events happening back home. These vivid scenes made Ezekiel feel as though he had transported physically from Babylon back to Jerusalem. Ezekiel chapter 8 always makes me cry with its vivid description of all the horrors happening in the temple. In my mind, I picture the majestic pageantry of the temple dedication service during King Solomon's reign, when God's glory filled the temple so completely that "The priests could not continue their service because of the cloud, for the glorious presence of the Lord filled the Temple of God" (2 Chronicles 5:14). The utterly desecrated temple Ezekiel viewed did not showcase any of God's glory. As Ezekiel approached the temple in his vision, he noticed a large idol beside the north entrance. This idol may have been an Asherah, the Canaanite goddess of fertility because King Manasseh had placed one there during his reign.[101] Then the Lord brought Ezekiel to the door of the temple courtyard where he saw a hole in the wall. The Lord told Ezekiel to dig into the wall where he found a hidden doorway. The Lord then instructed Ezekiel to go into this secret room. Ezekiel obeyed and "saw the walls engraved with all kinds of crawling animals and detestable creatures" (Ezekiel 8:10, NLT). This room also contained various idols being worshipped by seventy elders. Then the Lord brought Ezekiel to the temple's north gate where women were sitting, weeping for a false deity who represented fertile crops. As Ezekiel's vision concluded, the Lord took him into the temple's inner courtyard. "At the entrance to the sanctuary, between the entry room and the bronze altar, there were about twenty-five men with their backs to the sanctuary of the Lord. They were facing east, bowing low to the ground, worshiping the sun!" (Ezekiel 8:16, NLT).

These shocking revelations deeply disturbed Ezekiel as he pro-
cessed all he had seen and heard and then relayed it to the elders
and leaders sitting around him in his home in Babylon. I wonder
if Ishshah comforted him and held him close as he emerged from
his trance, overwhelmed with all he saw and heard. Ezekiel chapter
10 records God's glory departing from the Temple. What an inde-
scribable loss! I wonder if he awoke from that vision with tears running down his cheeks and his chest heaving under waves of crushing
sorrow. I also wonder if Ishshah's heart hurt for her husband as he
delivered such serious messages to the people and they responded
so callously. As the Lord told Ezekiel, "You are very entertaining to
them, like someone who sings love songs with a beautiful voice or
plays fine music on an instrument. They hear what you say, but they
don't act on it" (Ezekiel 33:32, NLT). The people came to gawk at the
show, but left unchanged.

Ishshah, along with the rest of the exiles, surely experienced long-
ings for her beloved homeland, as well as concern for friends and
loved ones left behind in Jerusalem. In addition, she may have wondered about family property in Israel and what was happening to it.
God had an answer for her and all the exiles, containing good news
and bad news. Whenever one of my daughter-in-law's little boys says,
"Mommy, I have some good news and some bad news," she always
says, "Well, give me the bad news first!" God gave the exiles the
bad news first when he told Ezekiel, "Son of man, the people still
left in Jerusalem are talking about you and your relatives and all
the people of Israel who are in exile. They are saying, 'Those people
are far away from the LORD, so now he has given their land to us!'"
(Ezekiel 11:15, NLT). We can imagine the impotent outrage this news
evoked! But then, God delivered the good news. "Therefore, tell
the exiles, 'This is what the Sovereign LORD says: Although I have

scattered you in the countries of the world, I will be a sanctuary to you during your time in exile'" (Ezekiel 11:16, NLT). The exiles who made God their Home, could experience comfort and peace as they released any expectation of recovering lost land. However, those who fixated on all they left behind, entertained bitter anger as they nursed plans for revenge. Sadly, we learn from reading Ezekiel that many of the exiles remained stubbornly rebellious as they continued to reject God's word to them.

One day, God said to Ezekiel, "'Son of man, you live among rebels who have eyes but refuse to see. They have ears but refuse to hear. For they are a rebellious people. So now, son of man, pretend you are being sent into exile. Pack the few items an exile could carry, and leave your home to go somewhere else. Do this right in front of the people so they can see you. For perhaps they will pay attention to this, even though they are such rebels. Bring your baggage outside during the day so they can watch you. Then in the evening, as they are watching, leave your house as captives do when they begin a long march to distant lands. Dig a hole through the wall while they are watching and go out through it. As they watch, lift your pack to your shoulders and walk away into the night. Cover your face so you cannot see the land you are leaving. For I have made you a sign for the people of Israel.' So I did as I was told. In broad daylight I brought my pack outside, filled with the things I might carry into exile. Then in the evening while the people looked on, I dug through the wall with my hands and went out into the night with my pack on my shoulder" (Ezekiel 12:2–7, NLT). When the people questioned the meaning of this elaborate visual aid, Ezekiel was commanded, "Explain that your actions are a sign to show what will soon happen to them, for they will be driven into exile as captives" (Ezekiel 12:11, NLT). Perhaps Ishshah helped her husband pack his small bag for this demonstration. Maybe it brought back memories of packing her own bag when she left home, one among many exiles taken captive to Babylon.

On another occasion, the Lord told Ezekiel to eat his bread with trembling and drink his water with quivering and anxiety. This also symbolized what would happen to the inhabitants of Jerusalem. As part of God's righteous judgment for their rebellious sin, the people would witness the horror of their cities laid waste and their land utterly desolated (Ezekiel 12:18–20). It would have been difficult to get some food and water down the hatch with all the excessive shaking. Maybe Ishshah's laundry loads increased during this time!

False prophets, male and female, complicated Ezekiel and Ishshah's difficult life even further as they habitually lied about visions from God to profit themselves. The Lord had very strong words for these charlatans leading so many astray. "Now, son of man, speak out against the women who prophesy from their own imaginations. This is what the Sovereign LORD says: What sorrow awaits you women who are ensnaring the souls of my people, young and old alike. You tie magic charms on their wrists and furnish them with magic veils. Do you think you can trap others without bringing destruction on yourselves? You bring shame on me among my people" (Ezekiel 13:17–19). Surely, Ishshah and her godly husband experienced great distress and discouragement as they witnessed the exiles' lack of discernment.

As Ezekiel, a true man of God, continued to deliver prophecy after prophecy, warning the people of impending doom, Ishshah stayed by his side. She had not bargained for this unusual life when she married Ezekiel, yet we know she continued to be a huge source of strength and support in his difficult and often misunderstood ministry. All along, Ishshah had stood by her man, watching all the drama unfold, unaware that God would use her sudden demise as the next object lesson to the hardened and rebellious people.

God spoke to Ezekiel one evening, telling him his wife would die the next day and that he must refrain from showing any grief over her death. "Son of man, behold, I am about to take from you the desire of your eyes with a blow; but you shall not mourn and you shall not weep, and your tears shall not come. Groan silently; make no mourning for the dead. Bind on your turban and put your shoes on your feet, and do not cover your mustache and do not eat the bread of men" (Ezekiel 24:16–17). "God revealed to the prophet that his wife would die suddenly and unexpectedly. The closeness of their relationship was heightened by the reference to her as the 'delight' of his eyes. She would be taken with 'one blow.' This usually described sudden death in battle or from plague or disease. Here it probably meant that she contracted some disease that was sudden and fatal."[102]

Fully obedient, in love with his wife, knowing she would soon be dead, Ezekiel announced Ishshah's impending death to the people in the morning (Ezekiel 24:18). Ishshah, as one of the people, would have listened in horror and then struggled with all sorts of emotions as she came to grips with the fact that she had only hours left to live. Ezekiel was approximately thirty-four years old during this event, so Ishshah would have been around that same age, in the prime of her life.[103]

I can't even begin to imagine the gamut and depth of Ishshah's emotions, certainly anger, fear, and grief among them. Perhaps the shock of it all made her numb. If they had children, she would have been scrambling to provide caregivers for them. If physically able, perhaps she sobbed her good-byes to friends and loved ones. If it were I, I would have clung to Ezekiel and begged him to ask God if there was any other way to get His message across. As the hours ticked down to her death, did she feel paralyzed by fear or had she resolved to die with dignity and grace. Or, if she contracted a disease that proved to be sudden and fatal, was she too sick to care?

My husband recently suffered an infection that led to sepsis. He quickly deteriorated and had to be transported by ambulance to the hospital. Had his sepsis not been effectively treated, he would have gone into septic shock. "Sepsis and septic shock can attack the young and the healthy. It is not uncommon for someone to seem completely well and normal one day, and be incredibly sick with sepsis, or even septic shock, 48 hours later. The risk of death is significant if sepsis leads to septic shock, with approximately 40% of septic shock patients dying, even with treatment."[104] We may wonder if perhaps Ishshah succumbed to something like septic shock with her sudden death.

Ezekiel faithfully obeyed God's instructions when his wife died. He showed no emotion; he stifled his deep groans of grief. He refrained from following any of his culture's grieving practices. He didn't cover his face; he didn't take off his shoes. In fact, he acted as though there had been no death in his family. Why? All along God had been warning His people through Ezekiel of the events that were now taking place. Because they had been so thoroughly warned, there should not have been much surprise. Furthermore, they had passively stood by while the temple in Jerusalem continued to be desecrated.

While Ezekiel grieved quietly and privately, he could be reassured that God shared his grief. Earlier, God had said to Ezekiel, "For I have no pleasure in the death of anyone who dies" (Ezekiel 18:32a). God felt no pleasure in Ezekiel's wife's death. We sometimes forget how deeply God sympathizes with our grief and other emotions. In fact, He feels them even more acutely than we do because He perfectly expresses all the emotions He created. May this truth comfort us when we are feeling crushed by the weight of our God-given emotions. We are never alone. Our Lord sympathizes with all our weaknesses because He experienced all of them while walking this earth as a fully sentient human being. Jesus, "tempted in all things as we are, yet without sin" (Hebrews 4:15), is the *most* sympathetic with our feelings. That's why we can "draw near with confidence to the throne of grace, so that we may receive mercy and find grace to help in time of need" (Hebrews 4:16).

God compared the death of Ezekiel's wife to the destruction of the beautiful temple. Just as God told Ezekiel that He was about to take from him the "desire of [his] eyes," so the people's desire of their eyes, the temple, would be taken from them. God told Ezekiel to tell the people that He was about to "take from them their stronghold, the joy of their pride, the desire of their eyes and their heart's delight" (Ezekiel 24:25). Just as the temple embodied all these things to the people, so did Ishshah to her husband.

Ishshah did not live to witness God removing her husband's semimuteness. God told Ezekiel, "As for you, son of man, will it not be on the day when I take from them their stronghold, the joy of their pride, the desire of their eyes and their heart's delight, their sons and daughters, that on that day he who escapes will come to you with information for your ears? On that day [the day of the temple's complete destruction] your mouth will be opened to him who escaped, and you will speak and be mute no longer. Thus you will be a sign to them, and they will know that I am the Lord" (Ezekiel 24:25–27).

Because Ishshah stayed with her husband, loving him, supporting him, and encouraging him throughout his unusual and difficult ministry, God could use this strong woman as a dramatic visual aid. In 586 BC, three years after the death of Ishshah, the takeover of Jerusalem was complete and the beautiful temple destroyed.

Everything God predicts always comes true because He is in complete control of the future and His perfect plans always come to fruition. "Not one of the good promises which the Lord had made to the house of Israel failed; all came to pass" (Joshua 21:45).

Scripture is full of strong women like Ishshah, but one of my personal favorites happens to be the sketch of the strong woman depicted in Proverbs 31. One writer noted "In English translations, this woman is deemed 'virtuous,' worthy, and of 'noble character,' yet none of these do justice to the original Hebrew—*eshet hayil*—which in fact means 'strong woman.'"[105] We may not be as strong, entrepreneurial, artistic, productive, or as wealthy as she, but this passage gives us permission to soar. This industrious woman used all the resources at her disposal to serve God, her family, and others. Instead of developing an inferiority complex by trying to compare our achievements or character qualities with hers, it helps to take a step back and look at the big picture of what she really modeled:

She cared for her husband by edifying him (31:12).
She cared for her family by feeding them (31:14–15),
She cared for her family by clothing them (31:21–22, 27a).
She cared for the poor by helping them (31:20).
She worked hard (31:13, 17–19, 22, 27b).
She used her money wisely (31:16, 24).

Now *that* is doable!

The word *husband* is mentioned three times in this Proverb, and I'd like to approach this text from a slightly different viewpoint—through the eyes of her husband. The three application points that follow will answer the question: How can we, as women who want to be strong and godly, honor our husbands in ways that glorify God?

Before we study the application points, however, may I encourage those of you who are currently single? Lest you be tempted to skip these principles because you think they could not possibly apply to you, hang with me! They do! The truth from Isaiah 54:4–6 is encouraging to all of us, "'Fear not, for you will not be put to shame; and do not feel humiliated, for you will not be disgraced; but you will forget the shame of your youth, and the reproach of your widowhood you will remember no more. For your husband is your Maker, whose name is the Lord of hosts; and your Redeemer is the Holy One of Israel, who is called the God of all the earth. For the Lord has called you, like a wife forsaken and grieved in spirit, even like a wife of one's youth when she is rejected,' says your God." These beautiful verses originally referenced Yahweh, Israel's covenant-keeping God, as He reassured His chosen people, but the principles of His love and faithfulness always hold true. Believing women who find themselves single or widowed, have a Husband who loves them perfectly and has redeemed them eternally. One day, all of us, as the Bride of Christ, will celebrate our union with Him when we partake in the marriage supper of the Lamb (Revelation 19:19). What a party that will be! The application points that follow are designed to help us become strong and godly women by God's grace and for His glory.

Trustworthy Women

We find the first mention of *husband* in Proverbs 31:11a. "The heart of her husband trusts in her." A husband's heart is strengthened when he can trust his wife; it's weakened when he cannot. Likewise, the hearts of our family members, friends, and coworkers are strengthened when we do things that increase, rather than diminish, their trust in us.

Ezekiel could trust Ishshah to stick by his side while he lay semi-conscious after visions, while he preached difficult messages of judgment, and while he acted out so many strange things. Repeatedly, as Ishshah proved her trustworthiness, Ezekiel's heart would have been strengthened. He could be proud of her and confident that she would continue to be a wife whom he could trust with anything.

I must confess I have not always strengthened my husband's heart by being a wife he could trust. Without Mark's wise balance, I can go overboard when it comes to being generous with our children and grandchildren. There have been times, to my great shame, when I've gone behind Mark's back to slip them some money without telling him. On one such occasion, I thought I'd do the right thing by asking him up front what he thought we should pay one of our boys for doing a one-time job for us. The amount he mentioned was not nearly as high as I thought it should be. So what did I, his "godly" wife do? I surreptitiously slipped this son some cash a few days before he did the work knowing Mark would give him a check for the amount he thought was best. My sin found me out for sure! When Mark handed him the check, our son responded with, "Oh, Mom already paid me!" Mark was disappointed and I felt horrible. I had broken trust with him.

As wives, we can break trust with our husbands in lots of ways: when we flirt with other guys, when we purchase an item and don't tell him or don't share the whole amount, when we criticize him in front of others or complain about him to others, when we undermine his authority as he's disciplining the children, when we belittle him or make fun of him, and so on. Every day is a choice to earn his trust in us or destroy it, to strengthen his heart or weaken it.

Ishshah proved to be the kind of wife who brought great delight to Ezekiel. A wife can make or break a husband. By being supportive of her husband and not leaving him once his difficult and unusual ministry began, Ishshah lent credence and respectability to Ezekiel in the eyes of the others. She proved she believed in his calling by choosing to support him.

Industrious Women

The second time the word *husband* is mentioned in Proverbs 31, it's in the context of a lengthy description of everything this woman achieves. We can feel intimidated and worn out just reading the list of all her accomplishments! She sounds like superwoman! We shouldn't feel disheartened if our achievements don't seem to measure up to hers. God grades on a different system than humans because only He can know, and therefore evaluate, the motives behind all our works and ways. First Corinthians 4:5 cautions, "So don't make judgments about anyone ahead of time—before the Lord returns. For he will bring our darkest secrets to light and will reveal our private motives. Then God will give to each one whatever praise is due" (NLT).

There's nothing wrong with receiving praise from others when they notice the excellence of our works and ways. However, the praise we receive needs to be redirected to reflect the God we serve as Matthew 5:16 reminds us. "Let your good deeds shine out for all to see, so that everyone will praise your heavenly Father." Ultimately, the praise we receive one day from God is what really counts for eternity.

Proverbs 31:23 states, "Her husband is known in the gates, when he sits among the elders of the land." This woman's husband enjoyed great respect from the elders because of the works and ways of his wife. Apparently, the community observed her industriousness, admired her business acumen, and noticed the ways she cared for her household, which reflected well on her husband and raised their level of respect for him.

As single women, we may not have an earthly husband who is praised in the gates for the kind of wife we are, but more importantly, we have a God who will be praised for the kind of believer we are. When we walk in close fellowship with Him and in obedience to His Word, His reputation is enhanced before a watching world.

Perhaps Ishshah became very creative with her handiwork as she tended to her homebound husband's needs. Perhaps she engaged in buying and selling and creating to help support her household. As the "desire of [his] eyes," Ishshah undoubtedly delighted her husband in all her ways.

Finally, let's examine the third time the word *husband* is mentioned in Proverbs 31. Her husband praises her saying, "Many daughters have done nobly, but you excel them all" (Proverbs 31:29). Her husband observed other women, and compared to his wife, they fell short.

Encouraging Women

Why does her husband issue such high praise? According to Proverbs 31:10, he had searched for, and found, a rare woman of virtue and high moral values to marry because he considered those qualities of greater value than precious rubies. "Who can find a wife of noble character? For her value is far more than rubies" (NET). He recognized that her noble character and high moral standards would influence her attitudes, words, and actions.

What about her attitude?

"Strength and dignity are her clothing, and she smiles at the future" (Proverbs 31:25). "The idea of clothing and being clothed is a favorite figure in Hebrew. It makes a comparison between wearing clothes and having strength and honor. Just as clothes immediately indicate something of the nature and circumstances of the person, so do these virtues."[106] When the storms of life hit, we have the impression that this strong woman rose to meet them head-on, instead of falling apart, because her strength ran deep, grounded in God.

As believers in Jesus, we know our strength comes from the Lord. I like how Psalm 18:39 depicts strength as clothing, "For You have girded me with strength for battle." God Himself is declared to be clothed with strength, "The Lord reigns, He is clothed with majesty; the Lord has clothed and girded Himself with strength" (Psalm 93:1). Not only is the Proverbs 31 Woman clothed with strength, she wears her dignity for all to see, making it easy to esteem and honor her.Clothed with strength and dignity, we perceive this woman as being thoroughly authentic, thereby earning high marks from her husband and others. She maintains a positive attitude and exudes strength, encouraging all whom she influences.

The second part of this verse shows how we can encourage others when it affirms, "she smiles at the future." Those of us for whom worry can weave its subtle tentacles into the fabric of our "clothing," can learn something from this girl! By smiling at the future, she is refusing to worry about it, or fear it. Most of what we worry about never comes true, and we can't get back all the time we wasted worrying over what turned out to be nothing. "Worrying is carrying tomorrow's load with today's strength. It is moving into tomorrow ahead of time. Worrying doesn't empty tomorrow of its sorrow, it empties today of its strength."[107]

When Mark and I lived in Dallas while he finished his doctoral course work at Dallas Theological Seminary, we resided in a little apartment close to the school. Mark worked part-time as an X-ray technologist at a local hospital. One afternoon, he neglected to come home at the usual time. As the hours passed, I gave in to full-blown worry. I tried to hide my panic from our three-year-old son, Josh, but failed miserably as the tears started flowing. I remember standing at the front window after having called all the hospitals—including the one where Mark worked—to see if he was in an emergency room due to a car accident, and anxiously willing his car to drive into our apartment parking slot.

When he casually walked through the door four hours later, I had mentally planned his entire funeral service, and how our little boy and I would move back to Arizona to live with my parents while I tried to raise him without his daddy. I was a complete mess. I didn't know whether to hug him or choke him when he finally arrived home! Mark explained he had lost track of time as he witnessed to a doctor with whom he had established a friendship. He walked into our apartment thrilled with the conversation they had, only to be confronted by a hysterical wife and frightened son. Of course, Mark felt horrible, apologized profusely, and promised never to do that again without letting me know. After I calmed down, and Mark shared all he and the doctor had discussed, I was able to rejoice with him at how God had directed his conversation with this agnostic doctor. All that needless worry certainly depleted my strength and I went to bed that evening, physically and emotionally exhausted.

Reflecting on the strength of Ezekiel's wife, there can be no stronger moment than when she listened to her husband deliver her death sentence. Instead of running away, if she had been physically able, she accepted her fate and became the ultimate visual aid for the destruction of the temple. Likewise, the Proverbs 31 Woman undoubtedly encountered her share of trials that always accompany life here on earth. Yet, based on how she is painted in Scripture, we perceive her as a strong, steadfast woman who enjoyed her present and smiled at her future.

What about her words?

"She opens her mouth in wisdom, and the teaching of kindness is on her tongue" (Proverbs 31:26). This woman's words are wise and encouraging. When our speech is governed by wisdom, we are prudent, knowing when to speak, when not to speak, and when we do speak, what to say. She is wise, loving, and kind; so much so, we have the sense that her first response is one of kindness. Because she embodies strength, dignity, confidence, wisdom, and kindness, she is more than qualified to instruct others.

This is very convicting! All too often, I speak silly or hurtful words that are devoid of wisdom. Sometimes I am appalled at what comes out of my mouth so quickly! I once walked into a hardware store to purchase an item I needed. While in the checkout lane, I noticed a packet of flower seeds I wanted, so I added them to my basket. For some reason, I only had cash with me that day and I didn't have enough for the flower seeds. When the cashier asked me how short I was, I blurted out the first thing that came to my mind, "five feet, four inches."

I recall one time, seated next to my mom's hospital bed, keeping her company, when my brother and his family joined us. As we sat around talking, I looked at my gorgeous, precious niece and blurted, "You're too beautiful for your own good." I shocked myself, and everyone in the room with those terrible words. My mother reprimanded me, her grown daughter, and I just wanted to become invisible. I apologized, but the damage was done.

Because I have often said hurtful, unkind, and foolish things to others, one of the constant prayers of my heart is Psalm 141:3, "Set a guard, O Lord, over my mouth; keep watch over the door of my lips." Once harmful words have escaped, there's no reining them back in or revising them. I need God's help every day to keep me from saying things I will later regret.

What about her actions?

"She looks well to the ways of her household and does not eat the bread of idleness" (Proverbs 31:27). This lady, who dressed well, had money to invest, sold items for profit in the marketplace, and employed a team of female servants, could have legitimately been idle. She could have reclined on her soft cushions and let others do everything for her. But we observe her incessantly thoughtful ways of caring for others. We discern her propensity to place the needs of others before her own. Her husband noticed all she achieved and praised her for doing everything with excellence.

I grew up in Argentina, South America, as the daughter of missionaries. Even though my mother employed a team of maids to help our family of seven with the washing, ironing, cleaning, and cooking, she refused to indulge in idleness. Instead, she labored just as hard as they did, right alongside them. She had a reputation for being wise and kind to all who were blessed to be in her presence and under her influence. I watched our series of maids fall in love with mom as she treated them more like daughters than hired help.

I believe Ishshah was the kind of woman who also displayed wisdom. She certainly made a wise choice to stand by her man in his most unusual and difficult ministry. His arduous mission could not rely on the positive receptivity of his audience because so many ridiculed his message and refused to believe his prophecies. He would have needed a wife who could speak lovingly to him, even though he could not verbally respond in kind.

My favorite verse in this passage is Proverbs 31:30, "Charm is deceitful and beauty is vain, but a woman who fears the Lord, she shall be praised." Why is charm defined as deceitful? When we look this word up in any dictionary, we find among the definitions allusions to magic and even witchcraft. It has the sense of tricking someone into believing something we're not.

In addition to charm, some rely heavily on outward beauty to get their way. But that can diminish as we age. Women who have defined their lives by others' response to their beauty, can start to panic and resort to surgical or chemical treatments to keep up the illusion of youth. We've all watched friends or relatives go under the knife, attempting to stave off the realities of aging. There is nothing wrong with having plastic surgery, but it is wrong when it becomes an all-consuming obsession that defines our sense of self–worth. Instead of striving to receive praise for outer beauty that can inflate vanity and quickly fade, we should focus on developing a passionate walk with God reflected in beautiful attitudes, kind words, and loving actions. That will bring lasting praise from God and others!

I would be remiss to not include my own mother in this chapter on strong women. I am blessed to have a mom who placed more value on developing her spiritual life than on enhancing physical attributes or accumulating material possessions. I am grateful for the ways she modeled humility in serving her Lord. She became fluent in Spanish so she could effectively share the gospel with people in Argentina and Venezuela. I am thankful for the cheerful ways she adjusted to challenging living conditions overseas. Her infectious laugh burst out so often, helping punctuate and lighten stressful situations. Her lack of pretension and gift of encouragement effortlessly drew others to her. Most of all, I am blessed with a mom who counted her walk with God and her knowledge of His Word as the most important pursuit of her life. With a cup of coffee, a well-worn Bible, an open journal, and a box of tissues nearby, my Mom treasured her daily visits with God.

So, what would you say Ezekiel's Ishshah, the Proverbs 31 Woman, and my mom have in common? What exactly made them strong, godly, and wise women? The answer lies in Proverbs 31:30, "a woman who fears the Lord." We may think the word "fear" belongs in a negative context. We may believe we're supposed to be afraid of the Lord, keeping our distance, fearful He could squash us flat any time we stepped out of line. That couldn't be further from the truth. Fear, defined biblically, is God-given, enabling us to reverence God's authority and obey His commandments.[108]

I realize the amazing blessing that was mine to have such a strong, godly woman for my mother. If Ishshah and Ezekiel had any children, they also would have benefitted from the influence of this strong, godly woman—especially as they observed the delight she brought to her husband. We know the portrait of the Proverbs 31 Woman includes children who are quick to praise her (Proverbs 31:28).

I recognize that some women, however, do not enjoy the privilege of having strong, godly women as mothers. For some, the friction they experienced during teenage years with their mothers only increased, and they remain semi-estranged. For others, their moms turned a blind eye to physical abuse going on in the home, destroying their daughter's trust in them. Still others have moms addicted to substance abuse and have little or no relationship with them. I don't know where you fall on the mother/daughter spectrum, but I do know that there are enough examples in Scripture, and in other strong, godly women we know, from whom we can learn and emulate. The great news is that we can start a new legacy by asking the Lord to help us become women who fear Him. We will be a true blessing to others, and most importantly, we will bring honor and glory to our God.

Father God, thank You for giving us a glimpse of Ezekiel's wife in Your Word. Because of her godly strength and faithfulness as she served alongside Ezekiel, You could use her death in such a dramatic and impactful way. We also thank You for the inspiring example of the woman depicted in Proverbs 31. Please help us be trustworthy, industrious, and encouraging women so that our lives will bless others and glorify You, I pray. Amen.

Focus Points

1. What are some things you could do to help foster your husband's or others' trust in you?

2. What are some things you need to stop doing, or refrain from doing, because they could destroy the trust placed in you?

3. Using the following columns, list some actions that can delight or disappoint your husband. If you are currently single, answer this using the Lord as your husband.
    Ways we can delight: Ways we can disappoint:

4. "An excellent wife is the crown of her husband, but she who shames him is like rottenness in his bones" (Proverbs 12:4).
    Complete the sentence as it relates to you: An excellent wife can be a crown for her husband by…
    Complete the sentence as it relates to you: A wife can shame her husband by…

5. To help us understand more clearly how to practically "fear the Lord," look up the following verses and note the accompanying benefits or cautions:
    Exodus 20:20
    Leviticus 25:17
    Deuteronomy 6:2
    1 Samuel 12:24
    Psalms 25:14
    Psalms 31:19
    Psalms 103:11
    Psalms 111:10

Proverbs 8:13; 14:26; 19:23

6. Often, when living with negative examples, we are motivated to do things differently. If you are a mother, or hope to be one someday, recalling your experience as a daughter, what would you change?

7. Now think about some positive examples you noticed as a daughter, and list what you would like to imitate and pass down to your own children.

VI

Gomer: Redeeming Romance

Ah! True love! What woman doesn't enjoy a good romantic story with a happily-ever-after ending? It doesn't hurt if it tugs at your heartstrings and makes you cry a little either! But fictional romance novels can also be subtly dangerous when they cause us to compare the too-good-to-be-true characters with the reality of our own lives. We may wonder, "Why can't my husband be like that guy?" or "Where's my Prince Charming?"

Flushed with love and starry-eyed, we view everything through rose-colored romantic glasses at the start of a serious relationship. But, once we're married, past the honeymoon, settled into a home, looking for employment, navigating the rapids of our relationship, raising children, and paying endless bills, our early euphoria is tempered by reality.

"A rather humorous and realistic picture of marital love was given in the *Saturday Evening Post* years ago, entitled 'Seven Stages of the Married Cold.' It goes like this:

First year: The husband says, 'Oh, sweetie pie, I'm really worried about those nasty sniffles you have! There's no telling what that could turn into with all the strep throat going around. I'm going to take you right to the hospital and have you admitted for a couple days of rest. I know the food is lousy there, so I'm going to bring you some takeout from China Garden. I've already arranged it with the head nurse.'

Second year: 'Listen honey, I don't like the sound of that cough. I've called the doc and he's going to stop by and take a look at you. Why don't you just go on to bed and get the rest you need?

Third year: 'Maybe you better go lie down, darling. When you feel lousy, you need the rest. I'll bring you something—do we have any canned soup around here?'

Fourth year: 'No sense wearing yourself out when you're under the weather. When you finish those dishes and the kids' baths and get them to bed, you ought to go to bed yourself!'

Fifth year: 'Why don't you take a couple of aspirin?'

Sixth year: 'You ought to go gargle or something, instead of sitting around barking like a dog!'

Seventh year: 'For Pete's sake, stop sneezing! Are you trying to give me pneumonia? You'd better pick up some tissues while you're at the store.'"[109]

At times, we may long for those early years of intense romance, sweet love notes, and focused attention. If we're single, we may feel the stinging lack of any romance right now. The good news is that we don't have to live without romance! God longs to be our one true

Love. He created us to fall in love with Him. He romances us in ways that humans never can. As we look at the book of Hosea, we will marvel at how God romanced His people Israel, and we will be astounded by Hosea's unconditional love and sacrifice for Gomer. Hopefully, we will have our hearts refreshed as we observe ways God romances us.

Before we meet Gomer, it's helpful to be aware of some major views regarding the biblical narrative of Hosea's marriage to her.

1. The story is not literal; it is simply allegorical.

2. Gomer was already a prostitute with children when Hosea married her.

3. Gomer was a typical young Israelite woman who had participated in a Canaanite rite of sexual initiation to prepare her for marriage.

4. It is a literal account. Gomer was sexually pure when she married Hosea and later became a prostitute.[110]

Many conservative theologians hold to the literal view of the story of Gomer and Hosea, that she was a chaste virgin when she married Hosea. One writer points out two main reasons for supporting this premise: As God's prophet, Hosea would have had a huge ethical and credibility problem marrying a known temple prostitute (2 Kings 17:13; 2 Chronicles 24:19), and Israel is referred to as being virginal when God began His love affair with her in the wilderness (Ezekiel 16:3–8).[111] In Hosea 9:10, the Lord says, "O Israel, when I first found you, it was like finding fresh grapes in the desert. When I saw your ancestors, it was like seeing the first ripe figs of the season" (NLT). This chapter will be based on view number four: The story of Hosea and Gomer is literal and Gomer was sexually pure at the time of her marriage to Hosea.

Whether she realized it or not, marriage to the prophet Hosea catapulted Gomer onto a public stage. Her life choices not only impacted her personal relationships, they also served as a mirror for Israel, reflecting the nation's relationship with their God. As Gomer's story unfolds, we will see that both she, and Israel, desperately needed God's redeeming romance.

In Gomer's day, Israel was divided into two kingdoms: the north, with Samaria as its capital, and the south, with Jerusalem as its capital. Gomer lived in the northern kingdom under Jeroboam II's reign. She grew up during a relatively prosperous, but unfortunately immoral period in Israel's history.[112] Her parents named her Gomer, the meaning of which implies to be filled up to the point of completion.[113] One hundred and fifty years before Gomer, one of Israel's king's, Jeroboam I, set up golden calves for the people to worship. This opened the floodgates to every evil expression of the Canaanite religion, including drunkenness, temple rites of prostitution, and even human sacrifice.[114]

Gomer's environment reflected her surrounding culture condoning pagan worship. Growing up in this rebellious climate dictated her mindset and colored her daily activities. One writer explains why the Israelites in Hosea and Gomer's day were so entrenched in this pagan lifestyle. "The attraction of Baal worship for the Hebrews went beyond immorality. It also included the promise of agricultural, animal, and human fertility. These fertility cults used sacred prostitutes, sexual activity, and imitative magic to insure fertility in every area of life. Baal worship was popular and difficult to eradicate from Israel because it fed on the people's lust, fear, and the desire to conform to their neighbors. It was encouraged by natural concerns for food, farms, families, and flocks, believing that Baal could help them insure the best in each of these areas. By embracing polytheistic forms of worship, the Hebrews conformed to the standards and lifestyle of their neighbors and thus created the social, moral, and spiritual problems that brought about their judgment."[115]

In Gomer's era, the Israelites had so intermarried and infused themselves into the Canaanite culture, they had even started calling Yahweh by the name of Baal, meaning "Lord" or "Master" (Hosea 2:16–17, NET).[116] Gomer would have been familiar with temple prostitutes called "holy ones."[117] As a young, impressionable girl, perhaps she marveled at the frenzied activities and garish parties accompanying Canaanite festival days. She may have looked upon the temple prostitutes as specially favored ones and perhaps even set her sights on becoming one herself someday. Perhaps she admired the attention they received, the clothes they wore, and all the gifts lavished upon them.

Sadly, the pervasive spread of idolatry had entangled so many of the daughters of Israel, and the rampant spirit of harlotry drew many into this pagan lifestyle. "For a spirit of harlotry has led them astray, and they have played the harlot, departing from their God. They offer sacrifices on the tops of the mountains and burn incense on the hills, under oak, poplar and terebinth, because their shade is pleasant. Therefore your daughters play the harlot and your brides commit adultery" (Hosea 4:12–13).

In God's providence, Gomer and Hosea's paths crossed. Perhaps she was a beautiful girl who stood out among her peers. Hosea knew her name, her family, and where she lived. Likewise, Gomer knew Hosea. They may have spoken the same language, but we may wonder if their upbringing and outlook on life differed greatly. Perhaps their interests were radically diverse as well. Given her actions as recorded in this book, it's highly doubtful Gomer shared Hosea's deep love for the God of Israel. Even though we don't know much about Hosea's upbringing or education, "his remarkable familiarity with the Torah, Joshua, and Judges suggests that he was thoroughly trained in the Scriptures (as they existed in his day). Similarly, the self-consciously enigmatic nature of his book suggests a high degree of intelligence and a subtle mind. We do not know how close he was to the political events of his lifetime."[118]

When Hosea first heard from the Lord, God addressed his singleness, and delivered clear instructions for marrying. "Go, take to yourself a wife of harlotry and have children of harlotry; for the land commits flagrant harlotry, forsaking the Lord" (Hosea 1:2). One writer noted that God's command to Hosea could be translated as "Go, take to yourself a wife who will prove to be unfaithful."[119] Another scholar commented that the Hebrew phrase for "wife of harlotry" means "promiscuous woman."[120] As was common among many young women growing up around pagan cultic practices, Gomer may have been disposed to favor that lifestyle.

We may wonder if Gomer and Hosea sensed an attraction between them when they married, or if Hosea went through the normal channels of participating in an arranged marriage, but what a heartbreaking prediction for Hosea! This girl he married could not be totally trusted. "Hosea was to be bound to this immoral woman in covenant union. For better or for worse, the path of his life would join hers. Hosea would be like Yahweh, who also bound himself in covenant with a willful and wayward people (Deuteronomy 9:6)."[121]

And yet, Hosea's love for Gomer may have been solid enough to overshadow the strong possibility of her future betrayal of their marriage vows. Young people tend to live in the present, and perhaps Hosea and Gomer experienced some enjoyable times together despite their differences and a thundercloud hanging over their heads. Like couples today, Hosea married Gomer for better or for worse. They bound themselves in a covenant union just as God had bound Himself in a covenant union with people who had proved to be unfaithful.

Not long after they married, Gomer became pregnant (Hosea 1:3). Imagine her joy at this evidence of fertility, especially considering her background ties to the Canaanite religion, which celebrated all things fertile. Did she credit Baal with her fertility? Imagine Hosea's exuberance when Gomer told him she was expecting their first child. Did he hope for a son to carry on his name and his allegiance to God? We know her pregnancy was successful because she delivered a healthy baby boy. And then for the second time in his life, Hosea heard directly from God (Hosea 1:4). The Lord told him to name the baby boy Jezreel, which in Hebrew means *God scatters*.[122]

It's important to place Hosea and Gomer's children in perspective as it relates to Hosea's ministry. "Hosea makes the births and naming of his children the beginning of the entire prophecy. He devotes more attention to their births than he does to his marriage to Gomer, and he records the significance Yahweh ascribed to each child's name. The children are themselves oracles, and they are the theological framework of Hosea's message. The report of their births should not be passed over as a sad but merely incidental prologue to the actual prophecy; *in a real sense, they are the prophecy, and everything else is just exposition.*"[123]

I wonder if pregnant Gomer tried out different baby names like moms do today? Was she disappointed in the name Hosea chose in obedience to God's word to him? Perhaps Gomer had heard all the horror stories associated with the name Jezreel. For example, the infamous Queen Jezebel was thrown down to her death from the palace window in Jezreel, instantly devoured by the city's wild dogs (2 Kings 9:30–36), and King Jehu killed King Ahab's seventy sons, piling their heads at the entrance to Jezreel's city gates (2 Kings 10:1–11). Gomer's beautiful baby boy's name recalled shame, judgment, and a bloody history. Did that make her sad? Did she resent Hosea's God? Was she embarrassed to tell her family and friends the baby's name? Did she hate that name? Gomer was on her way to discovering how it felt for her marriage and children to be object lessons for the divided nation.

It wasn't long before Gomer conceived once more. During her pregnancy, was she hoping for another boy or a little girl? Was she once again trying out baby names in the hopes that this time she could name the new baby? There are plenty of instances through-out Scripture where women named their children. After she gave birth to a sweet little girl, the Lord spoke for a third time to Hosea, instructing him to name his tiny daughter, Lo-ruhamah, meaning *she is not loved*.[124] It can also mean *no pity* (NET). The horrific name of their baby girl served as a stark warning to the people. The Lord told Hosea, "Name her Lo-ruhamah, for I will no longer have compassion on the house of Israel, that I would ever forgive them. But I will have compassion on the house of Judah and deliver them by the Lord their God" (Hosea 1:6–7). The people should have experienced intense fear and deep remorse upon realizing that God would withdraw His compassion from them because of their blatant disobedience and cal-lous disregard for Him. Did Gomer's heart break every time she held this little girl and called her *not loved*? Did she feel like saying to her, "I know that's your name, sweetheart, but please believe that I, as your mother, do love you"? Or was the shine beginning to wear off her marriage and was she becoming bitter as barriers built up around her heart?

After weaning her daughter, Gomer conceived again (Hosea 1:8). "It is curious that the text mentions the weaning of Lo-Ruhamah; it implies that Lo-Ammi was born some three years after Lo-Ruhamah since children nursed longer in the ancient world than today. It may be that Gomer lived faithfully with Hosea for a number of years."[125] However, as we read through the book of Hosea, we can observe that Gomer progressively became more alienated from her husband. She did not love his God and she didn't understand Hosea's ministry. Perhaps any feelings of love for her husband were dying within her, just like feelings of love for Yahweh were dying within the Israelites.

When Gomer gave birth to her second son and third child, the Lord spoke yet again to Hosea and told him to name the little boy, Lo-ammi, meaning *not my people* (Hosea 1:9, NET). God's people were not honoring their part of the covenant in the form of required obedience to God's laws so they could enjoy His blessing. By insisting on living in disobedience, they were certainly not acting like they belonged to Him.

Gomer's disillusionment led to dissatisfaction with her married life and she began to long for the carefree days of her past. The fleshly indulgences and glittering trappings of the Canaanite religion were strongly compelling her to listen to their siren song. The grass always looks greener on the other side of the fence. Gomer began to seriously contemplate leaving her husband and children and finding happiness outside the bonds of marriage, committing adultery with other men. Her selfish desire for her own pleasured fulfillment, her need to be free from life in a fishbowl, and the demands of three small children propelled her out of her house. What prompts a woman to be unfaithful? Many surface reasons, but bottom line—an emptiness she feels inside that she's desperately trying to fill. Gomer's very name *completion,*[126] which means fulfillment, did not ring true in her life.

After Gomer left home, Hosea faithfully delivered another message from God to His people. Doing so must have pierced his heart, because his sad situation mirrored the fractured relationship between God and His chosen people. "But now bring charges against Israel—your mother—for she is no longer my wife, and I am no longer her husband. Tell her to remove the prostitute's makeup from her face and the clothing that exposes her breasts (Hosea 2:2, NLT). "Some have interpreted this statement as a formal declaration of divorce, which is unlikely in this context. The Lord's ultimate purpose was to heal the relationship, not terminate it."[127] As another writer noted, this statement was probably an acknowledgement that "no reality remained in the relationship."[128] Gomer quickly slid into a reprobate lifestyle, as her adultery with other men became widely known. Likewise, Israel's fascination with pagan idolatry and participation in cultic rituals constituted spiritual adultery for her. Both Hosea and God were absolutely justified in bringing charges against Gomer and Israel.

Hosea distanced himself from his children for a time. He vowed, "I will have no compassion on her children, because they are children of harlotry. For their mother has played the harlot; she who conceived them has acted shamefully. For she said, 'I will go after my lovers'" (Hosea 2:4–5a). I wonder who stepped in to mother these three little ones during Hosea's absences. Unlike the prophet Ezekiel, who mainly ministered from his home, Hosea travelled the country delivering his messages. Maybe a grandmother, an aunt, or close family friend offered the children some stability and love during this difficult time.

Hosea's ministry did not cease with the infidelity and departure of Gomer. As one writer insightfully commented, "One would think that having the marriage collapse because of the wife's gross infidelity would be enough to disqualify anyone from claiming the role of God's spokesman. But the opposite is true. Hosea offers his private tragedies as his *credentials* for serving as God's spokesman. Hosea has endured as husband the same treatment God has endured as covenant Lord of Israel. More than any other, Hosea has the right to speak in God's name. He has shared in God's experiences and therefore can speak with God's heart."[129]

In chapter 2, Hosea eloquently expressed both his and God's feelings, experiencing a bride's unfaithfulness. In a series of "I will" declarations, God laid out a detailed plan of redemption and restoration for His beloved Israel. However, He first listed all the actions He would take to discipline His adulterous and rebellious bride. It's important to remember that God had given His people countless warnings through His prophets, and plenty of time to repent from their sinful ways and return to Him. God's discipline is always fair, timely, and warranted.

- I will strip her naked.
- I will expose her like she was when she was born.
- I will turn her land into a wilderness.
- I will kill her with thirst.
- I will have no pity on her children.
- I will fence her in with thorns.
- I will wall her in so that she cannot find her way.
- I will take back My grain during harvest times.

- I will take away My wool and My flax which I had provided to clothe her.
- I will expose her lewd nakedness in front of her lovers.
- I will put an end to all her celebration.
- I will destroy her vines and fig trees.
- I will turn her cultivated vines and fig trees into an uncultivated thicket.
- I will punish her for the festival days when she burned incense to the Baal idols (Hosea 2:3–13, NET).

Hosea 2:8 strikes a somber chord. "She doesn't realize it was I who gave her everything she has—the grain, the new wine, the olive oil; I even gave her silver and gold. But she gave all my gifts to Baal" (NLT). The people used God's gracious gifts to indulge in wickedness. They foolishly attributed their prosperity to Baal, instead of to the one true God, who alone provides every good gift (James 1:17). I marvel at how longsuffering God remained while His beloved Israel sank ever deeper into spiritual adultery.

God is love and He will never deny His nature and become capriciously unloving, even when He sometimes withholds His blessings so we can be disciplined by suffering the consequences of our disobedient actions. I love the next list of "I will" statements in Hosea chapter 2, because the day is coming when God will showcase His beautiful righteousness, justice, lovingkindness, compassion, and faithfulness to win back His beloved Israel. What a glorious example of a forgiving and redeeming God!

- I will allure her.
- I will lead her back into the wilderness and speak tenderly to her.

- I will give back her vineyards to her and turn the "Valley of Trouble" into an "Opportunity for Hope." There she will sing as she did when she was young, when she came up from the land of Egypt.
- She will call Me, "My husband."
- I will remove the names of the Baal idols from her lips.
- I will commit Myself to her forever.
- I will commit Myself to her in righteousness and justice, in steadfast love and tender compassion.
- I will commit Myself to her in faithfulness, then she will acknowledge the Lord (Hosea 2:14–20, NET).

In reading through the entire book, we learn that Hosea never stopped loving Gomer even though he suffered devastating pain and excruciating loss. Likewise, God never stopped loving Israel, even with the heartache they caused. As the prophet of his day, Hosea couldn't go away somewhere and hide, he still had to be on public display, even when shattered emotions impacted his thoughts and reflected on his anguished face. As he delivered God's word to the people, his heart would have resonated and identified with so many of the sad declarations.

Through Hosea, God told His people, "You have left me as a prostitute leaves her husband; you are utterly defiled. Your deeds won't let you return to your God. You are a prostitute through and through, and you do not know the Lord" (Hosea 5:3–4, NLT). Having firsthand knowledge of what this felt like would have given Hosea's speeches raw authenticity. He recognized that as Gomer went through lover after lover, deep down she was still empty inside, still unfulfilled. Likewise, Israel, pursuing other gods in a spirit of harlotry, kept chasing after the wind—never finding the true fulfillment their hearts desired.

And so Gomer lost herself in the frenzy of Canaanite cultic practices. As she immersed herself in this destructive lifestyle, Hosea threatened to publicly expose her for the travesty she had become, a woman going after all her lovers spurred on by physical lust and greed for material gain (Hosea 2:5–6). Gomer may have left her marriage tired of a life played out on a public stage, but unbeknownst to her, she was still on that public stage, acting as a powerful object lesson of Israel's own adultery in abandoning their God and lusting after pagan gods.

Embracing a sin-filled lifestyle, Gomer celebrated her new-found freedom to do whatever she pleased to satisfy all her desires. She may have thought that separating from a famous prophet would release her from being held accountable for her sinful actions. Perhaps Israel felt the same. But God said of His people, they "don't realize that I am watching them. Their sinful deeds are all around them, and I see them all" (Hosea 7:2, NLT). You may be familiar the cartoon character Pig-Pen in the old Charlie Brown movies. Dirt and dust inescapably swirled around his animated body, traveling with him wherever he went. That's what I picture when I read this verse, God viewing their sinful deeds swirling around them wherever they went.

Gomer's tragic story continues in Hosea 3. We find her in a pitiful state of degradation and despair. Several years had lapsed. Yet again, God spoke to Hosea, referring to him as a husband who still loved his adulteress wife. "Then the Lord said to me, 'Go again, love a woman who is loved by her husband, yet an adulteress, even as the Lord loves the sons of Israel, though they turn to other gods and love raisin cakes'" (Hosea 3:1). We may wonder "why Hosea describes Gomer in anonymous terms? The answer seems to be that she has forfeited her identity through her adultery. She can no longer claim the title 'wife of Hosea' just as Israel can no longer claim the title 'people of God.'"[130]

Without God-ordained grace on Hosea's part, this action could not have taken place. As one writer noted, "God has divorced Israel just as Hosea has divorced Gomer, but in both cases grace triumphs over righteous jealousy and the demands of the law. A man does not normally take back a woman who has behaved the way Gomer did. But we must acknowledge this as a revelation of grace through suffering."[131]

Perhaps Hosea had to go to the dirtiest, smelliest, parts of the city to track down Gomer and find the man who owned her. He ached to redeem Gomer. How many places did this man of God visit? How many people did this famous prophet approach to find out whether anyone had seen his wife? How much abuse did he receive from those who ridiculed or berated him? How many people strongly advised him to forget about Gomer, that she was a ruined woman beyond redemption?

Finally, Hosea found Gomer. What a scene that must have been! Her body had been used and abused too many times to count. She probably looked older than her years. She may have lost her beauty and no longer carried herself with any kind of pride. God said of His beloved Israel, "Worshipping foreign gods has sapped their strength, but they don't even know it. Their hair is gray, but they don't realize they're old and weak (Hosea 7:9, NLT). Gomer's pathetic physical condition reflected Israel's, spiritually speaking. Did Hosea's stomach clench with revulsion when he saw the state she was in? And Gomer, how could she even look her husband in the face knowing what she had become and what she had done? And yet, if she had dared lift her head for a fleeting glance, I believe she would have seen a love beyond explanation glowing in his eyes.

As Hosea negotiated with Gomer's owner, did she feel burning shame and bitter remorse? Or had she suffered so much abuse due to her own poor choices that she was simply numb? Was she glad her husband had found her or did she just want to die? "The circumstances surrounding this purchase are uncertain. Whether Hosea had legally divorced Gomer is unknown. She may have become a temple prostitute or was perhaps the legal property of someone who employed her as a concubine or hired her out as a prostitute."[132] Likewise, "The people of Israel have sold themselves—sold themselves to many lovers" (Hosea 8:9b, NLT). God lamented, "O people of Israel, do not rejoice as other nations do. For you have been unfaithful to your God, hiring yourselves out like prostitutes" (Hosea 9:1, NLT). The going price for a slave in those days was thirty pieces of silver. Hosea was not a rich man, but he did have fifteen pieces of silver, and seven and one-half bushels of barley, which sold for around fifteen pieces of silver.[133] Gomer's owner agreed to the transaction and the transfer was made (Hosea 3:2).

As Gomer followed Hosea home and they entered their neighborhood, did people peer out windows and doors trying to sneak a glimpse this notorious woman? Her sad saga had probably fanned the flames of town gossip for years. We can safely assume no "welcome home" party greeted her arrival into town. Her children were so young when she left, their memories of her fuzzy and faded. It's quite likely they were embarrassed by her and perhaps even ostracized because of her. The reunion between mother and children had to have been awkward with plenty of missteps.

Upon their return, Hosea set forth strict ground rules for Gomer. She was ordered, as his wife and purchased slave, to stay at home with him, sort of like house arrest. She was restricted from any involvement with other men. In fact, Hosea himself would refrain from having sexual relations with her for a prolonged period of time.[134] "You shall stay with me for many days. You shall not play the harlot, nor shall you have a man; so I will also be toward you" (Hosea 3:3). These rules were established to portray Israel's exile, when the people would be separated from their pagan idols and prohibited from participating in Canaanite religious practices (Hosea 3:4).

Hosea had mandated intimate physical distance between them, which would also have fostered emotional distance and filled the house with tension. It would have been natural for Gomer to "view her purchase by Hosea with terror. Would he now exact revenge on her as his slave? But Yahweh had commanded Hosea to love her, and Hosea gave her dignity, a new start, and an opportunity to regain her status as the prophet's wife."[135] Thankfully, Hosea remained committed to restoring his relationship with Gomer, just as God remained committed to restoring His relationship with Israel. I can't help but wonder if Hosea's heartbreaking experiences with Gomer granted him greater insight into God's heartbreak over the idolatry of His beloved people.

So how does Gomer's story end? I'd like to think that when she experienced Hosea's persistent love and unconditional forgiveness, she repented and reformed her adulterous ways, but Scripture doesn't tell us. I'd also like to think that her ending paralleled Israel's ending as described in chapter 14, since all along her story mirrored that of Israel's. Speaking of Israel's future restoration, the Lord promised, "I will heal you of your faithlessness; my love will know no bounds, for my anger will be gone forever. I will be to Israel like a refreshing dew from heaven. Israel will blossom like the lily; it will send roots deep into the soil like the cedars in Lebanon. Its branches will spread out like beautiful olive trees, as fragrant as the cedars of Lebanon. My people will again live under my shade. They will flourish like grain and blossom like grapevines. They will be as fragrant as the wines of Lebanon" (Hosea 14:4–7, NLT). I hope this resembled Gomer's ending as well!

If we are honest, all of us are Gomers. All of us are tempted to pursue things we think will complete or fulfill us. We may crave material possessions and try to amass as much as possible, seeking to become self-sufficient, envied by others, and cushioned in a cocoon of luxury. We may crave physical excitement and attempt to find it in illicit relationships or immoral ways. We may crave self-esteem and attempt to build it through calculated career moves or unabashed self-promotion. All these, and more, can be defined as idolatry—robbing God of our wholehearted love and devotion. When we place anyone or anything above Him and pursue anyone or anything more than Him, we become idolaters.

Sadly, even believers can bow to idolatry, just as Israel did in Hosea's day. Sometimes, even after being wooed by Him, we struggle with relinquishing control and yielding our will to His. We can buy into the lie that God is not enough, and His Word is not sufficient to meet all our needs. Like Gomer, all of us have sometimes taken selfish shortcuts to satisfy our fleshly desires, circumventing the spiritual maturity we would have gained by walking obediently in the Spirit. Because we're such needy human beings, we crave constant reassurance of unconditional and unfailing love; especially when life bombards us with all sorts of difficulties. Even as believers, we can begin to feel sorry for ourselves, unloved, and unappreciated. We can experience deep disappointment when loved ones let us down by not loving us perfectly enough, or meeting our needs often enough.

Thankfully, God, in His Word, is continually telling us how much He loves us. His love for us is perfect, unconditional, and everlasting. It's deeply reassuring to know that God will not love us any more once we are perfect, glorified, and in Heaven with Him, than He does now in our imperfectly human state. He is love. He never changes. His love for us is sourced in Him, not based on our merit or worthiness. He loves us perfectly because He is perfect love. How freeing to know there is nothing we need to do to earn His love!

Only God can love us perfectly by meeting every need and filling every void in our hearts. Only God can satisfy every longing of our souls. Only God can infuse our daily lives with joy and peace because of His matchless grace. When we trusted Jesus to be our Savior, we became the undeserving recipients of God's redeeming romance with us. As His beloved people, we are invited to experience full and complete satisfaction in our relationship with Him.

When my husband brings home a beautiful bouquet of flowers as an expression of his love for me, what if I said, "Oh, that's nice," but then left the bouquet on the kitchen counter, never unwrapping the cellophane and neglecting to place the flowers in water. I only fully appreciate his gift of love when I express my thankfulness by trimming the ends, carefully placing them in room temperature water, and adding that little packet of nutrients. Then I can enjoy the flowers and let them be a reminder to me of his love. It's the same with God's beautiful expressions of love throughout His Word. If I don't unwrap these gifts and let the words sink deep into my soul, fertilizing them with meditation, and obeying them through the power of the Holy Spirit, then I will never fully engage in a satisfying romance with Him. The following applications are intentionally worded with personal pronouns to encourage us to be deeply thankful for, and fully receptive of, His love for us.

God's limitless love for me makes me complete in Him.

> *"And may you have the power to understand, as all God's people should, how wide, how long, how high, and how deep his love is. May you experience the love of Christ, though it is too great to understand fully. Then you will be made complete with all the fullness of life and power that comes from God"* (Ephesians 3:18–19, NLT).

One day our youngest son, Jeremy, raced downstairs with a pressing question. He was in elementary school at the time and had learned a new word. He asked, "If you put a period behind the word *infinity*, will that make it shorter?" His young mind could not grasp an eternity without end. We have difficulty grasping the kind of love described in Ephesians. In fact, we need to ask God for the power to even understand the breadth and scope of His love for us. "The English words 'comprehend' and 'apprehend' both stem from the Latin word *prehendere*, 'to grasp.' We say that a monkey has a 'prehensile tail.' That is, its tail is able to grasp a tree limb and hold on. Our word *comprehend* carries the idea of mentally grasping something; while *apprehend* suggests laying hold of it for ourselves. In other words, it is possible to understand something but not really make it our own."[136]

Unlike human love, God's love for us knows no bounds and has no limits. He is romancing us right now with His limitless love. He wants us to not only understand (comprehend) His vast love, He wants us to experience (apprehend) His love in tangible, knowing ways. When we take our God at His word and resolve to apply His eternal truth to our daily life, we are apprehending His love for us. When we commit each concern to Him in prayer, trusting He will clearly direct our path, we are apprehending His love for us. When we acknowledge His involvement in every detail of our lives, we are apprehending His love for us. One of my favorite verses says, "The LORD directs the steps of the godly. He delights in every detail of their lives (Psalm 37:23, NLT). Our Romancer desires us to be filled to the point of completion with His love so that He is all we need.

God's permanent love for me keeps me safe with Him.

> *"And I am convinced that nothing can ever separate us from God's love. Neither death nor life, neither angels nor demons, neither our fears for today nor our worries about tomorrow—not even the powers of hell can separate us from God's love. No power in the sky above or in the earth below—indeed, nothing in all creation will ever be able to separate us from the love of God that is revealed in Christ Jesus our Lord"* (Romans 8:38–39, NLT).

Years ago, in teaching this verse to my Sunday school class of third and fourth graders, I needed an object lesson to help illustrate this truth. I remembered I had accidentally spilled superglue on a pair of utility scissors. The blades had stuck fast together. I had tried to pry them apart to no avail. Soaking them in boiling hot water, even dousing them in acetone, failed to separate the blades. So I brought the scissors to church and enlisted the help of two burly men. I explained what had happened to the scissors and that I couldn't separate the blades, but maybe the strong men could. I told them to pull on the scissor handles with all their might, secretly hoping the blades would stay stuck! Of course, they hammed it up as they each grabbed a scissor handle and pulled with all their might to try to separate the blades. Thankfully, for the sake of my crude illustration, they could not!

God's love not only fills us completely, it sticks to us like superglue and absolutely nothing seen or unseen can ever separate us from His love. His love binds us safely and securely to Him forever. As believers whose lives are hidden in Christ Jesus, there is nothing we could ever do that would make God stop loving us!

God's sacrificial love for me makes me precious to Him.

> "But now, O Jacob, listen to the Lord who created you. O Israel, the one who formed you says, 'Do not be afraid, for I have ransomed you. I have called you by name; you are mine. When you go through deep waters, I will be with you. When you go through rivers of difficulty, you will not drown. When you walk through the fire of oppression, you will not be burned up; the flames will not consume you. For I am the Lord, your God, the Holy One of Israel, your Savior . . . you are precious to me. You are honored, and I love you'" (Isaiah 43:1–4, NLT).

After God and His Word, there is nothing more precious to me on this earth than my husband, children, and grandchildren. When our oldest son, Joshua, was seven years old, we lost him for almost an hour. We were ministering in a camp setting in the pines of northern Arizona when he asked to join a group of kids exploring the nearby woods. Engrossed in play, the bigger kids accidentally left Josh behind. As any parent would feel who has lost a child, we were flooded with panic, desperate to find him. Thankfully, we recovered him, crying and scared, but physically unharmed. In a crisis mode, we develop tunnel vision and our mind laser-focuses on one thing—the precious treasure that's been lost.

When Hosea "lost" Gomer, we can sympathize with the range of emotions that must have flooded his soul. By divine design we are fully sentient beings created to experience every emotion in all its variances, just as God does, because we are created in His image. As ransomed believers in Jesus, and as beings created for His glory, we are God's precious children. How precious? May these eternal truths from Isaiah 43:1–4, soak into our souls: He created us. He formed us. He has ransomed us. He calls us by name. We belong to Him. He's with us as we navigate deep waters. He helps us keep our head above water when we swim in rivers of difficulty. He makes sure we're not burned to a crisp during fires of oppression. He is our Savior. As the undeserving, yet richly honored recipients of His sacrificial love, we are precious to Him.

God's comforting love for me gives me peace in Him.

> *"I am leaving you with a gift—peace of mind and heart. And the peace I give is a gift the world cannot give. So don't be troubled or afraid"* (John 14:27, NLT).

This verse is found within the context of some of Jesus's last words to His disciples. Soon, He would be leaving them physically, but He promised to send them the Holy Spirit to dwell within them, teaching them everything, and reminding them of all Jesus had taught them (John 14:26). In some translations, this verse refers to the Holy

Spirit as the Comforter. One writer noted, "In John chapters 14 to 16, we find Jesus, shortly before His arrest by the Jews, giving last minute instructions and comfort to his disciples. He was no longer going to be with them. They would indeed see Him again after His resurrection but only temporarily, till the ascension to His Father. The fact that Jesus would go to the Father would mean that they would be left alone, except if He sent a replacement, another one to fill in for Him. He was coming to them in 'another form' so to speak. And that's exactly what happened! Jesus, though no longer physically present, is much more present than before! How? Through the Comforter, the Holy Spirit; this Comforter truly fills in for Jesus, doing what He would be doing if He was physically present with each one of His disciples."[137]

As a little girl, I feared the dark. When night fell and shadows lengthened, I wanted to be inside the house with the lights on and near my parents. Even as an adult, I still notice a slight feeling of unease as nighttime falls. By the age of seven, I had three younger brothers and a baby sister. I remember Mom putting us to bed while Dad worked various night jobs to get through seminary and put food on the table. She would tuck us all in and then sit down at her piano to play us to sleep. As the music flowed all around us, I fondly recall the sense of peace and comfort that permeated our humble home. All was well with our little world.

Some years ago, Mark and I traveled to Israel on El Al Airlines. During takeoff, we noticed a young couple sitting in front of us, struggling to comfort their screaming baby. As the piercing cries continued and escalated, Mark and I mentally braced ourselves for a long and sleepless flight. Relief came in an unexpected way. An elderly lady made her way down the aisle to confront the couple.

After several minutes of a stern lecture delivered in Hebrew, punctuated with plenty of emphatic gestures, this older woman grabbed the baby, swaddled it tightly, and began rocking it back and forth while standing in the aisle. Almost instantly, the baby stopped crying and fell asleep. She then gave the baby back to the parents, delivered a few more choice words, and returned to her seat. I felt like applauding, but knew it would be inappropriate. Comforting the baby brought peace to everyone and we were grateful!

God's unfailing love for me gives me security in Him.

> *"But each day the Lord pours his unfailing love upon me"* (Psalms 42:8a, NLT).

As a child, my home in Argentina was simple and quite primitive. The bathroom and kitchen were housed in a separate building a short distance from the main house. We had no bathtub, only a shower. If we wanted to take a hot shower, we had to use a plastic bottle outfitted with a nozzle designed to pour kerosene directly into a trough surrounding the showerhead. We then lit the kerosene with a match, and while the flame burned inside the showerhead, we enjoyed hot water. Talk about timed showers! There was nothing worse than lingering too long in this shower and suddenly being doused with cold water—especially in winter. Today I am very grateful for hot showers that don't depend upon the contents of a small kerosene bottle, but I'm even more grateful for the uninterrupted flow of God's love pouring into my life. Isn't it wonderful and comforting to know that the flame of God's love never burns out?

The rest of this verse says, *"and through each night I sing his songs, praying to God who gives me life"* (Psalm 42:8b, NLT). The reason I can sing His songs in the night—in the dark times, the discouraging times, and the sad times—is because He is continually pouring His unconditional love into me, over me, and all around me.

God's unconditional love fills my heart with love for Him and for others.

> *"For we know how dearly God loves us, because he has given us the Holy Spirit to fill our hearts with his love"* (Romans 5:5, NLT).

I will never get over the wonder of God's love. He loved me before I even knew Him. He loved me as an unrepentant sinner. And then, when I began my relationship with Him, He gifted me with the indwelling Holy Spirit who fills my heart with His love. The love of God that surrounded me before I believed, is now inside, filling me completely! With His love filling our hearts through the power of the Holy Spirit, we're supposed to do two things: love God and love others as commanded in Matthew 22: 37–39, "You must love the Lord your God with all your heart, all your soul, and all your mind.' This is the first and greatest commandment. A second is equally important: 'Love your neighbor as yourself" (NLT). Isn't it great that God first fills our hearts with His love and then asks us to use that love, through the power of the Holy Spirit, to obey Him? He will always equip us before He asks something of us.

I'm learning to be grateful for the difficult people God allows into my life because it makes me painfully aware of my desperate need to love others with His unconditional love. My own human love is so fickle, conditional, and selfish. Being around those I don't enjoy, makes me want to distance myself from them, and quickly reveals the ugliness of my sinful human flesh. I'm slowly learning how to rely on the Holy Spirit to love the difficult ones through me. I'm learning to ask God to help me see them through His eyes of love, not my eyes of discriminating judgment. I'm discovering the relief and freedom of not having to rely on my feeble attempts to fulfill God's command to love them.

We don't know how Gomer's story ended. Did she find redeeming love, first in Hosea, and then in God? Did she experience Him filling all her empty spaces? We may not know the end of her story, but we can know the end of ours. If we follow our Lord faithfully and fruitfully to the end of our days, we will have enjoyed a redeeming romance that will continue without interruption throughout eternity.

Precious Father God, I pray that You will enable us to fully enjoy our redeeming romance with You, even before we get to heaven. I pray that we will experience, in the sweetest ways, all the facets of Your great love for us. How exciting to know that we get to continue the romance in heaven one day where our joy will know no earthly bounds and our hearts will be filled with an eternal capacity to reciprocate Your vast love for us. We are supremely blessed to be lavishly loved by You, the perfect Lover of our souls! Amen.

Focus Points

1. Second Corinthians 13:11 states, "Finally, brethren, rejoice, be made complete, be comforted, be like-minded, live in peace; and the God of love and peace will be with you."

   What are we promised when we are made complete in Christ Jesus?

   What other components accompany our completeness?

   It's not always easy to be like-minded and live in peace with others. Think of an instance when this was true in your life. How did God work in you, and through you, on that occasion?

2. Read Proverbs 18:10, then close your eyes and form a picture in your mind based on the truth of this verse. What are some fears you are facing right now?

   As you confess each fear, ask the Lord to be your strong tower and safe refuge, and thank Him for bearing your burdens by delivering you from debilitating fears.

3. Do you have a personal possession you consider precious? How do you take care of it? What precautions do you take for its safety? Why is it precious to you? As someone who is infinitely precious to God, name some ways He has taken care of you.

4. According to 1 Peter 1:18–20, we have been redeemed with something far more precious than silver and gold. With what were we ransomed?

   How is our life described before our ransom?

   What eventually happens to mere silver and gold?

   How long has God's ransom plan been in place?

5. Take some time for honest reflection by compiling a list of all the things that make you anxious, especially those keeping you awake at night!

6. Considering your list, read Philippians 4:6–7. Is there any item on your "worry list" that is excluded from the command in verse 6?

   When you commit your worries to the Lord, what should accompany your prayers?

   What are you promised in verse 7, after you have presented your requests to the Lord?

   Why is it so important that our hearts and minds be guarded by God's peace?

7. Psalm 91 is all about the security of one who trusts in the Lord. Take a moment to read this beautiful section of Scripture and then record some of the dangers listed in this passage.

   Are there any situations in your life that prompt insecurity? If so, what are they?

   Read Psalm 91 again and write down the phrases that describe our security in God.

   How will these truths help you the next time you are tempted to give in to your fears?

8. Jesus said, "Whoever has my commands and keeps them is the one who loves me. The one who loves me will be loved by my Father, and I too will love them and show myself to them" (John 14:21, NIV).

Based on this verse, how do we fully experience God's love for us?

9. God's love for us, and our subsequent love for others, is beautifully depicted in 1 John 4:7–12. As you read this passage, letting the words soak into your soul, is there a particular verse that captures your attention?
Which one and why?

10. According to verse 12, how is God's love made complete in us?

Notes

Chapter 1 Naomi: Seeking Security

1. Elisabeth Elliott, "Quotable Quote," accessed November 21, 2017, https://www.goodreads.com/quotes/298278-where-does-your-security-lie-is-god-your-refuge-your.

2. D. F. Payne, "Bethlehem" in *New Bible Dictionary,* 3rd ed. (Downers Grove, IL: InterVarsity Press, 1996), 133.

3. John W. Reed, "Ruth" in *The Bible Knowledge Commentary: Old Testament*, ed. John F. Walvoord and Roy B. Zuck (Wheaton, IL: Victor Books, 1985), 419.

4. Dale W. Manor, *Zondervan Illustrated Bible Backgrounds Commentary,* ed. John H. Walton (Grand Rapids, MI: Zondervan Publishing House, 2009), 246.

5. M. G. Easton, "Moab" in *Easton's Bible Dictionary* (New York: Harper & Brothers, 1893), Logos Bible Software.

6. NET Bible, note on Ruth 1:2 (Biblical Studies Press, 2005), computer file.

7. Ibid.

8. Ibid.

9. NET Bible, note on Ruth 1:4 (Biblical Studies Press, 2005), Logos Bible Software.

10. M. G. Easton, "Marriage" in *Easton's Bible Dictionary* (New York: Harper & Brothers, 1893), Logos Bible Software.

11. James E. Smith, *The Books of History: Old Testament Survey Series* (Joplin, MO: College Press, 1995), Logos Bible Software.

12. Brian Blum, "Roman vs. Jewish law: Whatever happened to patrilineal Jewish descent?," *The Jerusalem Post*, January 28, 2015, accessed December 4, 2017, http://www.jpost.com/Blogs/

This-Normal-Life/Roman-vs-Jewish-law-whatever-happened-to-patrilineal-descent-389254.

13. John W. Reed, "Ruth" in *The Bible Knowledge Commentary: Old Testament*, ed. John F. Walvoord and Roy B. Zuck (Wheaton, IL: Victor Books, 1985), 420.

14. M. G. Easton, "Chemosh" in *Easton's Bible Dictionary* (New York: Harper & Brothers, 1893), Logos Bible Software.

15. *New American Standard Bible: 1995 Update* (LaHabra, CA: The Lockman Foundation, 1995), note on Ruth 1:8, Logos Bible Software.

16. Kenneth L. Barker and John R. Kohlenberger III, *Expositor's Bible Commentary, Abridged Edition: Old Testament* (Grand Rapids, MI: Zondervan Publishing House, 1994), 369–70.

17. John W. Reed, "Ruth" in *The Bible Knowledge Commentary*, ed. John F. Walvoord and Roy B. Zuck (Wheaton, IL: Victor Books, 1985), 420.

18. Thomas L. Constable, "Notes on Ruth 1:14," in the NET Bible (Biblical Studies Press, 2005), accessed May 19, 2015, https://net.bible.org/#!bible/Ruth+1.

19. Kenneth L. Barker and John R. Kohlenberger III, *Expositor's Bible Commentary, Abridged Edition: Old Testament* (Grand Rapids, MI: Zondervan Publishing House, 1994), 369–70.

20. *New American Standard Bible: 1995 Update* (LaHabra, CA: The Lockman Foundation, 1995), note on Ruth 1:20, Logos Bible Software.

21. Daniel Isaac Block, "Judges, Ruth," in *The New American Commentary*, vol. 6 (Nashville: Broadman & Holman Publishers, 1999), 647.

22. *The Nelson Study Bible: New King James Version*, Earl D. Radmacher, et al. (Nashville, TN: Thomas Nelson, 1997), 444.

23. "Barley," Plant Site - Old Dominion University, accessed May 12, 2015, http://ww2.odu.edu/~lmusselm/plant/bible/Barley.php.

24. James M. Freeman and Harold J. Chadwick, *Manners and Customs of the Bible* (North Brunswick, NJ: Bridge-Logos Publishers, 1998), 201.

25. James E. Smith, *The Books of History: Old Testament Survey Series* (Joplin, MO: College Press, 1995), Logos Bible Software.

26. John W. Reed, "Ruth" in *The Bible Knowledge Commentary: Old Testament*, ed. John F. Walvoord and Roy B. Zuck (Wheaton, IL: Victor Books, 1985), 424.

27. NET Bible, note on Ruth 3:2 (Biblical Studies Press, 2005), Logos Bible Software.

28. John W. Reed, "Ruth" in *The Bible Knowledge Commentary: Old Testament*, ed. John F. Walvoord and Roy B. Zuck (Wheaton, IL: Victor Books, 1985), 424.

29. Daniel Isaac Block, "Judges, Ruth," in *The New American Commentary*, vol. 6 (Nashville: Broadman & Holman Publishers, 1999), 683.

30. NET Bible, note on Ruth 3:4 (Biblical Studies Press, 2005), Logos Bible Software.

31. Marjorie Bloy, "William Cobbett," accessed January 5, 2016, www.historyhome.co.uk/people/cobbett.htm.

32. NET Bible, note on Ruth 3:9 (Biblical Studies Press, 2005), Logos Bible Software.

33. P. A. Kruger, "The Hem of the Garment in Marriage: The Meaning of the Symbolic Gesture in Ruth 3:9 and Ezekiel 16:8," *Journal of Northwest Semitic Languages* 12 (1984), 86. Quoted by Thomas L. Constable in "Notes on Ruth (2017 Edition),"

accessed May 18, 2015, www.soniclight.com/constable/notes/pdf/ruth.pdf.

34. Daniel Isaac Block, "Judges, Ruth," in *The New American Commentary*, vol. 6 (Nashville: Broadman & Holman Publishers, 1999), 683.

35. Daniel Isaac Block, "Judges, Ruth," in *The New American Commentary*, vol. 6 (Nashville: Broadman & Holman Publishers, 1999), 691.

36. NET Bible note on Ruth 3:10 (Biblical Studies Press, 2005), Logos Bible Software.

37. George M. Schwab, "Ruth" in *The Expositor's Bible Commentary: Numbers–Ruth* vol. 2, ed. Tremper Longman III and David E. Garland (Grand Rapids, MI: Zondervan, 2012), 1336.

38. Thomas L. Constable, "Notes on Ruth 3:11," in the NET Bible (Biblical Studies Press, 2005), accessed November 15, 2017, https://net.bible.org/#!bible/Ruth+3.

39. Thomas L. Constable, "Notes on Ruth 3:15," in the NET Bible (Biblical Studies Press, 2005), accessed November 17, 2017, https://net.bible.org/#!bible/Ruth+3.

40. Jonathan Prime, *Opening up Ruth* in the *Opening up the Bible* series (Leominster: Day One Publications, 2007), 88.

41. D. R. W. Wood and I. Howard Marshall, *New Bible Dictionary*, 3rd ed. (Downer's Grove, IL: InterVarsity Press, 1996), 1022.

42. Charles R. Swindoll, "Ruth" in *The Historical Books*, accessed November 15, 2017, www.insight.org/resources/bible/the-historical-books/ruth.

43. NET Bible, note on Psalm 23:4 (Biblical Studies Press, 2005), Logos Bible Software.

44. Robert M. McCheyne, "I Am Debtor," in the *Scottish Christian Herald*, May 20, 1837.

Chapter 2 Hannah: Praying Power

45. Eugene H. Merrill, "1 Samuel," in *The Bible Knowledge Commentary: Old Testament*, ed. John F. Walvoord and Roy B. Zuck (Wheaton, IL: Victor Books, 1985), 433.

46. NET Bible, note on 1 Samuel 1:2 (Biblical Studies Press, 2005), Logos Bible Software.

47. Stelman Smith and Judson Cornwall, *The Exhaustive Dictionary of Bible Names* (North Brunswick, NJ: Bridge-Logos, 1998), 193.

48. G. T. Manley, "Eli," in *New Bible Dictionary,* 3rd ed. (Downers Grove, IL: InterVarsity Press, 1996), 310.

49. Ibid.

50. J. W. Meiklejohn, "Hophni and Phinehas," in *New Bible Dictionary,* 3rd ed. (Downers Grove, IL: InterVarsity Press, 1996), 480.

51. Robert D. Bergen, "1, 2 Samuel" in *The New American Commentary*, vol. 7 (Nashville: Broadman & Holman Publishers, 1996), 67.

52. "Jehovah Sabaoth - LORD of Hosts," Precept Austin, last modified December 10, 2017, accessed September 26, 2015, http://www.preceptaustin.org/jehovah_sabaoth_-_lord_of_hosts.

53. Robert D. Bergen, "1 and 2 Samuel" in *The New American Commentary,* vol. 7 (Nashville: Broadman & Holman Publishers, 1996), 67.

54. Robert D. Bergen, "1 and 2 Samuel" in *The New American Commentary,* vol. 7 (Nashville: Broadman & Holman Publishers, 1996), 69.

55. NET Bible, note on 1 Samuel 1:19 (Biblical Studies Press, 2005), Logos Bible Software.

56. M. G. Easton, "Samuel," in *Easton's Bible Dictionary* (New York: Harper & Brothers, 1893), Logos Bible Software.

57. Robert D. Bergen, "1 and 2 Samuel" in *The New American Commentary,* vol. 7 (Nashville: Broadman & Holman Publishers, 1996), 72.
58. Margaret Tolliver, editorial comment, March 20, 2015.
59. Robert D. Bergen, "1 and 2 Samuel" in *The New American Commentary,* vol. 7 (Nashville: Broadman & Holman Publishers, 1996), 81.
60. Daniel B. McGee, "Ephod" in *Holman Illustrated Bible Dictionary* (Nashville, TN: Holman Bible Publishers, 2003), 499.
61. Robert D. Bergen, "1 and 2 Samuel" in *The New American Commentary,* vol. 7 (Nashville: Broadman & Holman Publishers, 1996), 79–80.
62. Ibid.
63. NET Bible, note on 1 Samuel 2:5 (Biblical Studies Press, 2005), Logos Bible Software.
64. Corrie ten Boom, "40 Powerful Quotes from Corrie Ten Boom," accessed December 6, 2017, https://www.crosswalk.com/faith/spiritual-life/inspiring-quotes/40-powerful-quotes-from-corrie-ten-boom.html.
65. P. L. Tan, *Encyclopedia of Illustrations: Signs of the Times* (Garland, TX: Bible Communications, Inc., 1996), 1046.

Chapter 3 Abigail: Pleasing God

66. Stelman Smith and Judson Cornwall, *The Exhaustive Dictionary of Bible Names* (North Brunswick, NJ: Bridge-Logos, 1998), 179.
67. Robert D. Bergen, "1, 2 Samuel" in *The New American Commentary*, vol. 7, (Nashville, TN: Broadman & Holman Publishers, 1996), 245.

68. Kenneth L. Barker and John R. Kohlenberger III. *Expositor's Bible Commentary, Abridged Edition: Old Testament* (Grand Rapids, MI: Zondervan Publishing House, 1994), 423.

69. Robert D. Bergen, "1 and 2 Samuel" in *The New American Commentary,* vol. 7 (Nashville: Broadman & Holman Publishers, 1996), 245.

70. Kenneth L. Barker and John R. Kohlenberger III, *Expositor's Bible Commentary, Abridged Edition: Old Testament* (Grand Rapids, MI: Zondervan Publishing House, 1994), 423.

71. Ibid.

72. Robert D. Bergen, "1 and 2 Samuel" in *The New American Commentary,* vol. 7 (Nashville: Broadman & Holman Publishers, 1996), 250.

73. Robert D. Bergen, "1 and 2 Samuel" in *The New American Commentary,* vol. 7 (Nashville: Broadman & Holman Publishers, 1996), 250.

74. James E. Smith, "1 & 2 Samuel" in *The College Press NIV Commentary* (Joplin, MO: College Press Publishing Company, 2000), 303–4.

75. Stelman Smith and Judson Cornwall, *The Exhaustive Dictionary of Bible Names* (North Brunswick, NJ: Bridge-Logos, 1998), 49.

76. Thomas L. Constable, "Constable's Notes," in the NET Bible (Biblical Studies Press, 2005), accessed November 16, 2017, https://net.bible.org/#!bible/Galatians+1.

77. Robert P. Lightner, "Philippians," in *The Bible Knowledge Commentary: New Testament,* ed. John F. Walvoord and Roy B. Zuck (Wheaton, IL: Victor Books, 1985), 653–54.

78. Thomas L. Constable, "Constable's Notes," in the NET Bible (Biblical Studies Press, 2005), accessed September 30, 2014, https://net.bible.org/#!bible/2+Corinthians+5.
79. Mark Hitchcock, *The End: A Complete Overview of Bible Prophecy and the End of Days,* (Carol Stream, IL: Tyndale House Publishers, 2012), 218.
80. Stelman Smith and Judson Cornwall, *The Exhaustive Dictionary of Bible Names* (North Brunswick, NJ: Bridge-Logos, 1998), 3.

Chapter 4 Bathsheba: Finding Forgiveness

81. Stelman Smith and Judson Cornwall, *The Exhaustive Dictionary of Bible Names* (North Brunswick, NJ: Bridge-Logos, 1998), 33.
82. Margaret M. Tolliver, editorial comment, September 24, 2015.
83. D. W. Baker "Uriah" in *The New Bible Dictionary*, 3rd ed. (Downers Grove, IL: InterVarsity Press, 1996), 1219.
84. Robert D. Bergen, "1 and 2 Samuel" in *The New American Commentary,* vol. 7 (Nashville: Broadman & Holman Publishers, 1996), 365.
85. Ronald F. Youngblood, *The Expositor's Bible Commentary,* ed. Frank E. Gaebelein et al., vol. 3 (Grand Rapids: Zondervan Publishing House, 1991), 933.
86. Kenneth L. Barker and John R. Kohlenberger III *Expositor's Bible Commentary, Abridged Edition: Old Testament* (Grand Rapids, MI: Zondervan Publishing House, 1994), 294.
87. Robert D. Bergen, "1, 2 Samuel" in *The New American Commentary*, vol. 7, (Nashville, TN: Broadman & Holman Publishers, 1996), 368.

88. Robert D. Bergen, "1, 2 Samuel" in *The New American Commentary*, vol. 7, (Nashville, TN: Broadman & Holman Publishers, 1996), 369.

89. Miriam Feinberg Vamosh, *Women at the Time of the Bible* (Herzlia, Israel: Palphot Limited, 2007), 43–44.

90. Corrie Ten Boom, "I'm Still Learning to Forgive" accessed December 20, 2017, https://www.guideposts.org/better-living/positive-living/guideposts-classics-corrie-ten-boom-on-forgiveness.

91. Robert Jeffress, *How Can I Know: Answers to Life's 7 Most Important Questions* (Brentwood, TN: Worthy Publishing, 2012), 174.

Chapter 5 Ezekiel's Wife: Being Strong

92. Wayne A. Grudem, ed., *Biblical Foundations for Manhood and Womanhood* (Wheaton, IL: Crossway Books, 2002), 83.

93. Stelman Smith and Judson Cornwall, *The Exhaustive Dictionary of Bible Names* (North Brunswick, NJ: Bridge-Logos, 1998), 73.

94. Charles H. Dyer, "Ezekiel," in *The Bible Knowledge Commentary: Old Testament,* ed. John F. Walvoord and Roy B. Zuck (Wheaton, IL: Victor Books, 1985), 1225.

95. Lamar Eugene Cooper, "Ezekiel" in *The New American Commentary,* vol. 17 (Nashville, TN: Broadman & Holman Publishers, 1994), 19.

96. Lamar Eugene Cooper, "Ezekiel" in *The New American Commentary,* vol. 17 (Nashville, TN: Broadman & Holman Publishers, 1994), 59–60.

97. Ibid.

98. Ibid.

99. Ralph Alexander, *Ezekiel* (Chicago, IL: Moody Press, 1976), 18.

100. Ibid.

101. Charles H. Dyer, "Ezekiel," in *The Bible Knowledge Commentary: Old Testament,* ed. John F. Walvoord and Roy B. Zuck (Wheaton, IL: Victor Books, 1985), 1243.

102. Lamar Eugene Cooper, "Ezekiel" in *The New American Commentary,* vol. 17 (Nashville, TN: Broadman & Holman Publishers, 1994), 239.

103. "Ezekiel Bible Timeline," Bible Hub, accessed August 6, 2015, http://www.biblehub.com/timeline/ezekiel/1.htm.

104. Jennifer Whitlock, "Sepsis and Septic Shock: Understanding the Differences," last modified April 14, 2017, accessed November 27, 2017, https://www.verywell.com/sepsis-and-septic-shock-3156848.

105. Miriam Feinberg Vamosh, *Women at the Time of the Bible* (Herzlia, Israel: Palphot Limited, 2007), 6.

106. NET Bible, note on Proverbs 31:25 (Biblical Studies Press, 2005), Logos Bible Software.

107. Corrie ten Boom, *Clippings from My Notebook* (Nashville, TN: Thomas Nelson Publishers, 1982), 33.

108. D. R. W. Wood and I. Howard Marshall, *New Bible Dictionary* (Downers Grove, IL: InterVarsity Press, 1996), 365.

Chapter 6 *Gomer: Redeeming Romance*

109. David S. Thompson, *Twelve Biblical Steps to a Successful Marriage* (Xulon Press, 2009), 60–61.

110. Robert B. Chisholm Jr., "Hosea" in *The Bible Knowledge Commentary: Old Testament*, ed. John F. Walvoord and Roy B. Zuck (Wheaton, IL: Victor Books, 1985), 1379.

111. Leon J. Wood, "Hosea" in *The Expositor's Bible Commentary,* ed. Frank E. Gaebelein et al., vol. 7 (Grand Rapids: Zondervan Publishing House, 1985), 164–66.

112. D. R. W. Wood and I. Howard Marshall, *New Bible Dictionary* (Downers Grove, IL: InterVarsity Press, 1996), 557.

113. Stelman Smith and Judson Cornwall, *The Exhaustive Dictionary of Bible Names* (North Brunswick, NJ: Bridge-Logos, 1998), 89.

114. James Orr, "Definition for BAAL" in *International Standard Bible Encyclopedia*, accessed December 20, 2017, http://www.bible-history.com/isbe/.

115. Lamar Eugene Cooper, "Ezekiel" in *New American Commentary*, vol. 17 (Nashville: TN: Broadman & Holman Publishers, 1994), 26–27.

116. NET Bible, note on Ezekiel 2:16 (Biblical Studies Press, 2005), Logos Bible Software.

117. Claude Mariottini, "Canaan in Patriarchal Times" *Biblical Illustrator Magazine* (Fall 2000), 3–10.

118. D. A. Garrett, "Hosea" in *The New American Commentary,* vol. 19 (Nashville: Broadman & Holman Publishers, 1997), 22.

119. Robert B. Chisholm Jr., "Hosea" in *The Bible Knowledge Commentary: Old Testament*, ed. John F. Walvoord and Roy B. Zuck (Wheaton, IL: Victor Books, 1985), 1379.

120. D. A. Garrett, "Hosea" in *The New American Commentary,* vol. 19 (Nashville: Broadman & Holman Publishers, 1997), 51.

121. Ibid.

122. Ibid., 55.

123. M. G. Easton, "Jezreel" in *Easton's Bible Dictionary* (New York: Harper & Brothers, 1893), Logos Bible Software.

124. D. A. Garrett, "Hosea" in *The New American Commentary,* vol. 19 (Nashville: Broadman & Holman Publishers, 1997), 69.

125. Robert B. Chisholm Jr., "Hosea" in *The Bible Knowledge Commentary: Old Testament*, ed. John F. Walvoord and Roy B. Zuck (Wheaton, IL: Victor Books, 1985), 1381.

126. G. W. Grogan, "Gomer" in *New Bible Dictionary*, 3rd ed. (Downers Grove, IL: InterVarsity Press, 1996), 423.

127. Robert B. Chisholm Jr., "Hosea" in *The Bible Knowledge Commentary: Old Testament*, ed. John F. Walvoord and Roy B. Zuck (Wheaton, IL: Victor Books, 1985), 1383.

128. Derek Kidner, *Love to the Loveless: The Message of Hosea* (Downers Grove, IL: InterVarsity Press, 1981), 27.

129. D. A. Garrett, "Hosea" in *The New American Commentary,* vol. 19 (Nashville: Broadman & Holman Publishers, 1997), 49–50.

130. Robert B. Chisholm Jr., "Hosea" in *The Bible Knowledge Commentary: Old Testament*, ed. John F. Walvoord and Roy B. Zuck (Wheaton, IL: Victor Books, 1985), 1387.

131. D. A. Garrett, "Hosea" in *The New American Commentary,* vol. 19 (Nashville: Broadman & Holman Publishers, 1997), 99.

132. Ibid., 49.

133. Robert B. Chisholm Jr., "Hosea" in *The Bible Knowledge Commentary: Old Testament*, ed. John F. Walvoord and Roy B. Zuck (Wheaton, IL: Victor Books, 1985), 1387.

134. Ibid.

135. D. A. Garrett, "Hosea" in *The New American Commentary,* vol. 19 (Nashville: Broadman & Holman Publishers, 1997), 104.

136. Warren Wiersbe, *The Bible Exposition Commentary*, vol. 2 (Wheaton, IL: Victor Books, 1989), 33.

137. Anastasios Kioulachoglou, "Panting After God (Holy Spirit: 'Another Comforter')," last modified August 4, 2015, accessed August 17, 2016, http://wmcgrew.blogspot.com/2015/08/holy-spirit-another-comforter.html.

Because of the dynamic nature of the Internet, any web address or links listed in the endnotes may have changed since publication and may no longer be valid.

About the Author

Barby Bailey grew up in Argentina as the daughter of missionaries. She has enjoyed a life of service opportunities as a pastor's wife, seminary president's wife, and elementary school teacher. In addition, she considers it a great privilege to continue to share God's Word at conferences, retreats, and in church settings. Her experience leading and participating in numerous Bible studies has made her an excellent student of God's Word. Her many trips to Israel have helped her form a clearer picture of the history, geography, and culture of the women she writes about.

Barby and her husband, Mark, have been married for forty-five years. They have two sons.

Made in the USA
San Bernardino, CA
18 May 2019